"We trained hard, but it seemed that every time we were beginning to form up into teams, we would be reorganized. I was to learn later in life that we tend to meet any new situation by reorganizing; and a wonderful method it can be for creating the illusion of progress while producing confusion, inefficiency, and demoralization."
. . . Gaius Petronius Arbiter, Roman Satirist, 210 BC.

While likely a false citation, it is at least known to have been said much later by Charlton Ogburn, Jr. (1911-1998).

It is not important who first uttered this cogent thought. When a business is not organized in such a way as to allow you to work efficiently and effectively, it has failed to make working what it should be. At the same time, when you don't clearly know what your work is, how to improve it, and how to work as an individual and within a team, both you and the business suffer. This book is designed to help you and the organization understand how to achieve optimal work and continuous improvement.

Danny Langdon
Originator of the Language of Work™
Business Consultant, 2018

THE
WORKING
MODEL

F O R   W O R K E R S

T H E

WORKING
MODEL

USING THE LANGUAGE OF WORK
TO IMPLEMENT WORK

BOOK 3 OF THE WORK TRILOGY

DANNY G. LANGDON
KATHLEEN S. LANGDON

© 2018 Performance International

Published by:
Performance International
5 Oval Court
Bellingham, WA 98229 USA
360-738-4010
www.performanceinternational.com
info@performanceinternational.com

ISBN Paperback: 978-0-9913975-9-4
ISBN eBook: 978-0-9913975-6-3

The Language of Work™

The Language of Work™ (LoW) is a systemic, enterprise-wide system for organizing, managing, implementing, and continuously improving work by means of powerful integration tools. This goal is achieved through the universal use of a Work Formula that is applied through a process known as Work Analytics to a series of integrated Work Implementation Models. While that sentence is a mouthful, this book turns it into a series of easily understood, illustrated pieces.

The anchor of the Language of Work is the Work Formula: a behaviorally based, clear reflection of work using a standard formula to apply various Work Analytic Tools. Its use allows:

- executive management to provide everyone with a shared understanding of the business mission, ultimate goals, and ongoing objectives;
- managers to effectively facilitate employee achievement; and
- workers to do their parts individually and in teams by thoroughly understanding work and committing to its continuous improvement and overall implementation.

Every business consists of people and jobs at all levels of the organization. Communication within and between these levels is paramount to business success. The three Work Implementation Models of the LoW are an excellent method of addressing this basic quality of business. A separate book is devoted to each one:

The Business Model

Primarily for executives, this book demonstrates how to organize a business to achieve work alignment, operational transparency, and continuous improvement. The model applies to all four levels where work is planned and accomplished. Ways to align organizational needs related to standards, work support, human relations, and financial support are also provided. The book is also recommended reading for managers and workers who want a complete understanding of the Language of Work as it relates their role in the business as a whole.

The Managing Model

Primarily for managers, including team leaders, this book explains how the Language of Work, through Work Analytic Tools, can facilitate various management functions to achieve continuous work improvements. The Managing Model is a logical, systemic extension of The Business Model. Thus, what the executive develops through The Business Model managers can effectively facilitate using the same Work Formula. The book will also be of interest to workers aspiring to a managerial role.

The Working Model

Primarily for workers, this book shows how to use the Language of Work Formula to implement and continuously improve work as an individual worker and as part of a team. Using a variety of Work

Analytic Tools, individuals and teams can work together to meet executive and management work goals. Using the Work Formula they learn how to continuously improve work to maximize work effectiveness, efficiency, and to effect needed changes as they are planned by management. Managers will want to read this book to support their facilitation of work.

Each of the three books in *The Work Trilogy* is written for a specific audience; each is independent, and yet all three comprise an integrated system. To make each book stand alone, a certain amount of redundancy is needed. We trust the reader of two or all three of the books will not find this bothersome. As with any new language, the Language of Work demands practice and repetition. Deeper insights can occur as one reads again, learning the many nuances of this new way to look at and practice the work of business.

As you learn new ways, the authors hope you will share that knowledge with us, and we welcome questions as you use the Language of Work.

Danny and Kathleen Langdon

The Working Model:
A Book for Job Holders
and Teams

By virtue of the commitment to either *The Business Model* and/ or *The Managing Model,* your company will be employing the Language of Work to more fully understand and improve work at all levels of the organization. Even if your company has yet to commit to the deployment of the LoW Model, you are probably interested in improving your work on your own. *The Working Model* is designed to assure your optimal work performance.

This book is designed to empower you to take charge of your job and maximize your team participation so that you can more completely fulfill your own potential. This will help contribute to your overall success and to that of the business. In addition to improving your own work, you can use this model to ease any angst you may feel during needed change.

This book will expand your thinking and approach to work. You will be able to apply a new insight to your job and to working with others. You can expect the following from reading this book:

1. Clarify your tasks through application of a Work Formula, relating the formula to work execution whether as an individual or as part of a team.
2. Enhance your relationships with colleagues and managers so that your work is the best for others' use and vice versa.
3. Enable better planning and implementation.
4. Continually improve, and freely adapt to change.

We expect that this book will change how you perceive your job and your relationship with coworkers and management. You will find ways to be more effective, to reduce discomfort, to increase personal satisfaction, and to enjoy being part of a team. In addition to making you and your company better, this book should also help position you to advance your career.

Used in concert with the two other books of the *Work Trilogy*, *The Working Model* advances work excellence. It does so by using the universal Work Formula introduced in *The Business Model* to organize the work, and in *The Managing Model* to facilitate clear definitions and alignment of that work. The three models of *The Work Trilogy* provide a business with a total system that can successfully integrate the efforts of executives, managers, and workers by creating and using a shared Work Formula—giving your company a true Language of Work.

Danny Langdon
Originator of the Language of Work
Performance International
5 Oval Court, Bellingham, WA 98229
www.performanceinternational.com

Contents

Acknowledgements

We want to thank in the broad sense all the people who, over two decades of development, have so generously given of their time and thoughts in enhancing the application and refinement of the Language of Work.

Thanks first to several executives, managers, and workers with whom we have had the pleasure of working as consultants. Their ideas and suggestions were very instrumental in keeping *The Work Trilogy* centered on real-world needs and circumstances. Thanks to Roby James, our copyeditor, for helping us to communicate effectively our Language of Work. Thanks to Brittney Langdon for final proofing.

And special thanks to our "third-party" readers—Joanna Berg, Meg Lang, and Brenda Sample—who worked so diligently to find any last minute, glaring illustration or reading issues. Very special thanks to Ghislain Viau, Creative Publishing Book Design for working with us on cover designs, print and eBook formatting. With so many at-the-last minute edits and changes on three books at the same time he was very patient and extremely professional.

Danny and Kathleen Langdon

Preface

Everyone has their own perception of the work of an organization, and that is precisely the problem with work. One sees it by the org chart, others by function, or by the jobs and teams, and still others by the processes. Or worse yet, we only see the enterprise in terms of what we do. It's time for a common way to view business, understand how to improve it where needed, manage and do our work in concert with that shared understanding. That is where the Language of Work comes into play.

While we were writing this book, we often had conversations with a wide range of friends, colleagues and clients, who inquired about the subject of the book as part of the Trilogy of Work. As soon as we revealed the working title and basic content, the universal response was a not-so-unexpected, "Boy! Could my current (or former) company or department use this kind of systematic approach to understanding and organizing business!" Nearly everyone thinks businesses could be run better; they also agree that organizations are rarely defined and understood well. We have helped facilitate several organizations using the LoW and confirmed that it works. It will work for you!

Danny and Kathleen Langdon

Chapter 1

Work as Workers See It

People make a choice when it comes to how they view work. That choice affects their perspective. One way is to just accept work as it is given. Another is to add a personal spin to it. For example, a bus driver or cabbie just collects money, drives a route, and receives a paycheck (and in the case of a cabbie, a tip). Or a bus driver can view the job as an opportunity to make people a little happier. She still collects fares, drives the route, and collects a paycheck. But she also greets each passenger with a big smile and a comment, helps people with change, gives walking directions, tells stories, provides history, and allows moms with babies and people with canes or bikes the time they need to board safely. That's adding a personal spin to work.

> How workers view work affects how they conduct their jobs. Some usual ways of looking at work are reviewed, and then possibilities are raised for a better way!

Others use a variety of techniques learned through various courses, certifications, and degrees. A hairdresser might suggest a cancer check to clients. A software programmer might add web searches or virus checks to each project. These are good and represent a very personal perspective on work. But there are typically only a few who truly understand what comprises work in a behavioral sense.

If you ask people what they think about their work, here are some of the answers you might hear:

- Work sucks!
- Work is a four letter word!
- Work would be fine if I didn't have to deal with customers.
- Work would be fine if I didn't have a boss.
- I could never do your job!
- It's hard!
- Well, I have to listen to people all day who I am sure don't like me.
- I can't wait to retire.
- I love my work!
- I get to do things all day long that I enjoy.
- I love the people I work with . . . we are like family!

These are either praise or complaint, but all without task-related content. The worker in a collections call center makes a negative observation. The head of a nonprofit might be more satisfied with his job and therefore praise it. But each of these is an ordinary observation and lacking in information that would give insight into the work itself.

Others might offer more meaningful responses:

- I approach my work with an algorithm in my head. In other words, I am going to do this, then that, followed by such and such!
- I approach my work the way a firefighter would…I relax until a crisis comes, and then I fix it.
- I just look at work as a big project…and think like a project manager.
- I am a chef, so I think about flavors and presentation and how to use ingredients that I can get a hold of and make magic.
- I keep a list of tasks in my head—and do the ones I don't like so much first, and then attack ones I like later in the day.
- I make lesson plans every week, and then gather my materials before school, and start the lesson that I planned.
- I check the calendar—it tells me what programs I need to plan, who the speakers are and what I need to do.

Those responses suggest to a listener a deeper knowledge of what a job entails. Still other respondents focus on marshalling their personal traits as part of their work, such as:

- I just need to have enough energy and nerve to get there and do my duties.
- I am very extroverted, so I talk to people at the office, on the phone first, and then when I have been energized by them, I go to thinking about the work I have to do.
- I am a problem solver, so I look at the problem from every angle and then figure out how to respond to it.
- I am a researcher, so I follow the trails that the research presents to me until solutions present themselves.

Yet others might describe a process they follow:

- I take notes on everything I read, and then sort them out and start writing/acting on them.
- I check in with my team to see what's happening, and do what they think I should do.
- I wait for my boss to tell me what's up today—then I do it.
- I learn what my job will look like when I attend the shift meeting…and learn what happened last night and what has to be taken care of today.
- I think a lot at night before I go to work, so when I get there, I have pretty well decided what the next step is.

Those groups of statements could be called the three Ps of work: Planning, Personality, and Process. Each of these is good, well-intentioned, and shows a proactive insight in the approach to work, even though each is very different. However, because each is based on personal preference, conflicts are bound to occur. The planners will get upset with the personality-focused folks. The process-oriented people will think the planners are procrastinating, and the personality-driven folks will tend to disrupt the others. This is the reason there are so many management and supervision courses on working with difficult people, Meyers-Briggs Type Indicator training, and conflict management. What if all three of these types, (and any others not mentioned here) could all have a clear definition—that they have created and agreed on—of the work they do?

What if it were possible to lay out graphically and simply, in a systematic way, all the human elements a job encompasses, from the doer herself to her suppliers and her customers, both inside and outside the company?

What if there is a work system that is easy to understand, to share, to change, and to build on? What if it would create a more proactive, clear, and systemic approach to what every employee will do as an individual and as a team member?

What if, rather than relying solely on one's own best efforts and/ or a scattering of isolated, learned practices/principles/methods, you could understand all work behavior—everyone else's, as well as your own? Would this reduce workplace drama and discomfort? Would it allow everyone to improve daily work?

The authors have developed a universal systems approach based on behavioral principles that can be viewed and acted upon in a cause-and-effect way—the Language of Work Model. Its Work Formula, a means to achieving organization, management, and implementation, as well as to meeting work challenges, provides a valuable add-on to your current perception of work. It allows everyone to establish and act upon work in a common way that helps build on shared concern and practices about work. To understand and do so requires a profound understanding of what work is!

We will therefore begin by defining work.

Chapter 2

What Is Work?

Given that we all work—and generally we do a lot of work—it might seem odd to begin with the question of what work is. You would think that, from all our work experience, we must surely be able to define "work." We do work forty or more hours a week, month after month. We may have been doing a particular job for twenty years or more. We constantly talk about work with others. Surely we know what work is!

Surprisingly, our experience with thousands of people at all levels of business has revealed that there is no *common* way to define (and therefore to talk about, plan, change, or generally deal with) work. This isn't to say that it is impossible for individuals to talk about *their* work. All of us have a technical language (finance, electronics, insurance, retail,

> We begin to understand work in terms of its dependent and interactive elements. This leads to a highly useful "Work Formula," to use for organizing, facilitating, implementing, and improving work. Each worker can understand their work and communicate better with others.

manufacturing, banking, etc.), and we seem to be able to communicate, to varying levels of completeness and clarity, *about* our work and, to some degree, that of others who share our industry. However, when we get together to organize, facilitate, implement, or improve work—identify and agree on what is wrong with it, how to make it better, what needs to change—we find people just don't look at or talk about work the same way.

For example, when a team leader asks, "How are the six of us going to approach solving a work problem [such as how to add a new software feature to our current system]?" you can readily picture three to perhaps six different approaches to this challenge. Each person has a different idea of what is needed and the process to use. This gap means we do not have the right words to discuss work or evaluate ways to make it better. There hasn't been, until now, a common "Language of Work." We introduce one here and show the many ways it can be used by you, your team, management, and your whole business.

To have a "language," we need a lexicon. But simply "making things clearer" through more words is not sufficient. When asked what work is, most say that work is a series of tasks or activities to accomplish a goal. But that definition lacks precision as applied to the work of each individual or team. So descriptive phrases as to what work is do not suffice. Rather, we need to have a functional, interactive model to structure, clarify, communicate, and apply daily in terms of work. We need something of a structure—something analogous to what we understand as the structure for composing a sentence—on which to hang a common meaning of work. If we don't, we will continue to experience frustration and drama in the workplace when it comes to describing virtually any work. A few typical work problems will serve to demonstrate the need for a highly functional Language of Work everyone can use.

- Nobody tells me when a change occurs.
- Too many people think they can do my job.
- Nobody cleans up after themselves. I hate coming in to work and finding a mess, left over from the day before.
- Why do we always run out of toner around here?
- Why do I have to use my own cash to get supplies? And wait weeks for reimbursement?
- I have too much work to do—there are not enough hours in the day!
- There are too many interruptions around here.
- I have to be back-up for the receptionist—makes me crazy!
- Execs are always telling us to do more with less—but they don't understand how complicated it is.
- Getting permits out of the city takes way too long.
- Calculating the taxes in every different place we work takes too long.
- I have to hound people for their timesheets—but I need them to do payroll!

You can begin to see from these examples that if we do not have a way to achieve agreement about what presently exists as work, we cannot envision with others what *should* exist to make things better. Thus, work enhancement and change are impossible, even if critical. Nor can we identify and agree on the exact nature of any actual problems we know exist. Instead, we are left to argue—based on individual perspective—what a problem is and how to address it. This involves a lot of guessing and expensive changes made through trial and error. Furthermore, without agreement on what the work is and where the problem lies, we cannot evaluate the various solutions offered for change, either in advance or afterwards.

Change is one of the most important tools in the life of any business, but commitment to change is frequently missing or confusing. We either don't understand the nature of a needed change or the reason behind it, or we are not committed to the change because we were not involved in helping to decide on it. Thus, organizations end up using a variety of approaches to improving or changing work. Businesses often end up throwing out several solutions to see if one is actually used by workers. Many times these random solutions are less than optimally functional or take an inordinate amount of time and cause employee confusion and angst.

Before defining work, we need to recognize that work is a *shared* process, not just what an individual does. Therefore work must be defined, committed to, and implemented not only up, down, and across an organization, but with suppliers (internal and external) and customers. To do this, we need a way to describe work that allows every point of view and every required need to be universally acknowledged and interwoven. While that may seem at the same time too simple or too daunting—or even naïve—we ask that you try what we suggest in the context of your individual work and with your team. As have so many others, you will begin to see results—both big and little.

What Therefore Is Work?

Possible answers to: "What is work?" might seem as simple as, "It's the activity we engage in," or "It's what I get paid to do," or "It's what makes money for the company." These typical responses are true, but very limited. They do not provide any functional understanding of the complexities of improving work performed alone or with others.

It's kind of like saying water is wet without understanding that water is actually H_2O—something which all scientists understand. That shared understanding enables them to see it the same way, to explore what to do with it—like study its properties, combine it with other compounds, develop new uses for it, and so on. Mere descriptions of what work is miss important elements that provide a full definition and understanding of work. We need to include everything people might answer when asked what their work is, as well as describe how each element relates to other elements in a cause-and-effect manner.

We will now ask a series of questions in a particular order, from which we can create a template of the parts of work that can be assembled (or populated, to use a common management term) to meet various business needs, starting with, for the sake of simplicity, your own job. We will use that template to derive a Work Formula that can be repeatedly re-created. In this book of *The Work Trilogy*, we are addressing work exclusively at the individual and team level. In other parts of the trilogy, we address the whole organization (the work of executives) and managing (the work of managers).

The following questions will help us arrive at a complete, highly useful, and easily understood model of work. Answer these questions first for yourself about your own job. Later, work with your team to answer these same questions to define the work of your group (team, unit, department, etc.):

For the individual:

1. Can you name deliverables that you are expected to produce?

2. Can you state the "value" or impact your deliverables will have for you, customers, and the business as a whole?

3. Can you explicitly identify what will initiate your work and list the resources needed to produce your deliverables?

4. Do you know what internal rules and/or external regulations affect how you do the work?

5. Can you list the steps or procedures you use to achieve your outputs and consequences?

6. Do you know if mid-course corrections in your work are needed, and how do you know when the work is done satisfactorily?

For the team you are part of:

1. Can you name deliverables that your team is to produce?

2. Can you state the "value" or impact your team's deliverables will have for you, your customers (internal and/or external), and the business as a whole?

3. Can you explicitly identify what will initiate your team's work and list the resources needed to produce the deliverables?

4. Does the entire team know what internal rules and/or external regulations impact how you do the work?

5. Can you list the steps or procedures your team uses to achieve the outputs and consequences?

6. How does your team know if mid-course corrections in the work are needed, and how do they know when the work is done satisfactorily?

If you have any doubts about any of the answers—yours or the team's—your understanding and execution of work is, to one degree or another, jeopardized. Furthermore, even the answers to each question would be incomplete if you didn't know the inter-relationship of those answers and how they impact one another when not done correctly or efficiently.

The answers to these questions will form a fundamental, behavioral understanding of work that impacts you and those you work with, as well as those who manage you. Having clarity on the answers and their cause-and-effect relationship will go a long way toward improving your work performance and that of your group. Answering these six questions precisely, and connecting the answers to each other, introduces a succinct, easy to understand and apply Work Formula. That formula will lead to an operational understanding of work that can allow you, your organization, and its management a more effective route to success.

What Are the Six Elements That Define Work? What Is Their Cause-and-Effect Relationship?

1. Do you and the team know exactly what deliverables are to be produced?

   We have consistently seen bewilderment on the faces of workers, including managers and executives, when we ask the first question about work, which can also be phrased, "What do you produce?" Eventually, someone will finally mention one item and then another; sometimes we have to probe with an additional question, "Who are your clients/customers, and what are the tangible products or services you provide them?"

   You might think that everyone in the organization could readily spell out what they produce, but if you ask them directly, you are likely to receive a disparate set of answers, often composed of the steps leading to a deliverable, rather than the deliverable itself.

   Why is this key question about the output of work often so hard to answer? Perhaps it is just easier to focus on the *activity* in which we engage, rather than what we actually produce. We address this latter aspect of work shortly, but now need to be clear about the tangible products (reports, artifacts, programs, etc.) each worker or team produces. Rarely do we think of the result/the output/the deliverable to our customer, client, or colleague as a key element of our work. In fact, we often forget completely about our internal or external customers. Whatever the reasons, clarity on the outputs (or deliverables) a person or team is expected to produce is critical to our understanding of what work is and how it can be improved.

2. Can you state the "value" or impact your deliverables will have for you, customers, and the business as a whole?

   Knowing *why* you are doing the work is intrinsic to achieving both personal goals and business expectations. Can you state explicitly the impact your work is to achieve? Indeed, can you link the outputs with their effect—on you personally, on other employees, on your internal and external clients, and on the business as a whole? Being specific is important. "Achieving world peace," for example, is far too broad, as is "ending hunger." They may be worthwhile goals, but they do not describe anything about an organization's day-to-day activities. So "produce profit" doesn't work either. The impact of what you produce (what value you add) needs to be measurable. Then, and only then, is it a part of the definition of work. We will come to refer to the concept of "adding value" as "consequences," a behavioral term and one which, in business, should be positive.

   You'll additionally note that we began with the introduction of outputs and consequences to link their systemic relationship: each individual or team output or deliverable at work should contribute to the impact or value of specific organizational deliverables.

3. Can you explicitly identify what will initiate your work and list the resources needed to produce the deliverables?

   This may be the easiest question for everyone in the workforce to answer. We have a pretty good idea of what we need to do our work in the way of resources, such as specific data, physical tools, other people, facilities, funds, and so forth. However, one of the more critical inputs in the identification of our work is often overlooked: These are the "triggers" (events or people) which cause the work to begin. This includes specific requests, orders, etc., from clients, as well as manager's requests or previously established schedules. Thus, there are two types of "inputs" to be aware of in the definition of work—resources and triggers.

4. Do you and the team know what internal rules and/or external regulations impact how you do the work?

    Many workers and managers don't spend time thinking about how their work is governed by policies and rules that come from inside the organization or laws and regulations from outside. Perhaps they become aware of them only when they get into trouble for not following them. Some governance for jobs—such as safety regulations—is obvious. Others may not seem so apparent. Company policies on treatment of employees (such as HR law, Fair Labor Standards Act, labor contracts, ethics rules) must be known and adhered to by employees and managers alike. Success at work requires compliance with all pertinent guidelines. Some organizations provide training on such rules, but others create a landmine for employees and managers to traverse. Some rules are mandatory and must be readily available or repeatedly discussed in training sessions. Upon occasion, we have found organizations where all the rules were under lock and key, creating a major obstacle to the definition and execution of work. We call any rules and regulations the "conditions" of work.

5. What steps or procedures do you use to achieve the outputs and consequences?

    The steps needed to produce an output are generally well known, but may not be commonly agreed on by workers and managers.

    In our work modeling, we have seen two extremes when it comes to articulating process: on the one hand, no general procedures exist, so no process maps are available. People do their jobs based on a common assumption about the work. They may have "grown up" in the organization and therefore seem to understand what is going on. We also see organizations where every single process is mapped, often in excruciating detail. Both of these extremes share a common problem: the connection between the core processes and the tasks of a job is unclear at best. And when changes are instigated, the changes often create confusion. Process steps need to be defined at a level for practical use, but not so rigidly as to rule out necessary changes. Additionally, we need to understand the relationship between outputs and consequences—how they are achieved by using inputs and how they are informed by the conditions of work.

    Some may not understand how what they do impacts others' work. The questions for them are: "Are the steps you normally perform understood by people in other parts of the organization?" "Are there circumstances under which changing steps is called for when conditions dictate it?" Some people we've encountered feel that asking about process is asking about a procedure manual or about job descriptions, but in actuality we seek a view of the steps designed for overall communication, clarity and consensus. If the organization needs greater detail, that can be incorporated in another document.

Because the process steps take the inputs, follow the conditions, and produce the outputs, which are linked to the consequences (impact), an understanding of the systemic relationship between the work elements develops automatically. But there is one additional element to a complete Work Formula that must be included.

6. How do you know if mid-course corrections in your work are needed, and how do you know when the work is done satisfactorily?

No other element of work is more often missing than what we label "feedback." Neither managers nor workers regularly get the level of feedback they need to assure they are doing their work correctly and completely. Rather, most feedback comes in negative terms as a response to failure. Businesses rarely ask for feedback without associated negativism.

To avert this, the Language of Work articulates the sources of feedback that should be used to determine if the process is proceeding smoothly or needs to be corrected. At the end of the process, what mechanism is used to signal that the work is done? Even moderate clarification or use of certain feedback can lead to marked improvement in job, team, and management performance. In general terms, you can think of feedback as the various kinds of communication—verbal and nonverbal—that exists or should exist to help us make mid-course corrections in our work and let us know we have achieved what needs to be achieved.

The Interaction or Systemic Features of a Work Formula

Once you have clear answers to the questions above, you can begin to explore the second major characteristic that makes for a useful Work Formula: that is, the behavioral interaction of these elements of work and how that interaction becomes a scaffold for modeling work and doing numerous other things. This behavioral interaction tells you how work happens (or doesn't) and how to organize, manage, implement, and change it. Since you both work with and are managed by others, knowing the interaction of the work elements allows you to identify the effects of changes in any element, as well as the effect on others. (For example, a change in a rule or condition can and often does affect the process.) You will be better able to identify where problems exist, arrive at solutions to reduce or eliminate them, and more easily implement strategic or technological work changes. As a result, everyday performance will improve, sometimes dramatically.

In the chapters which follow, we introduce the Work Formula of the Language of Work Model as the foundation to *The Work Trilogy*. We shall also introduce a variety of ways to apply this Work Formula through what we refer to as Work Analytic Tools.

Chapter 3

The Work Formula

So far, we have introduced the idea that to accomplish work most effectively—particularly with others—you need to have a common, shared understanding of what the work actually *is*. Further, to understand what the work actually is, you need to agree on the elements of work, see how those elements relate to one another and to the accomplishment of results, and how knowing the elements will help improve or change work. Without this shared understanding, you invariably end up with many personal opinions or power struggles that make consensus hard, if not impossible. When more complex questions arise—such as how to organize, implement, change, and manage work—the issues and problems caused by different understandings of work are magnified.

> We introduce a systematic and systemic Work Formula to help you understand and implement your individual and team work. Thus, everyone will share a common Work Formula to unify and share their understanding, consensus, and execution of work.

Let us begin by looking at a simple example.

21

Suppose one person says that work shared with other employees is defined as "winning proposals" (which is a consequence), while a second says it is defined by "the customer" (who is important, but an input and the ultimate receiver, rather than a consequence). A third employee says work is "hard," which is a descriptor, but not a definer of work. Yet another might say it all about process. Each fiercely supports his or her position, often leading to misunderstanding, conflict, lack of consensus, or fragmented commitment, none of which leads to discernible improvements in the work.

Contrast this to what occurs when the *definition* of work includes all the elements we briefly introduced in Chapters 1 and 2. Then, by defining the actual work (such as what would lead to a winning proposal) with all interested parties, you can achieve shared clarity on any given aspect of the work at hand. There will be no drama, no conflict, just a clear picture—a model—of the work. Put another way, if you think work is composed of two elements, but I think it has six elements, and someone else thinks there are three, we are in trouble from the outset.

Imagine what that confusion is like when multiplied by tens or hundreds of workers, managers, and executives of any organization. Only when everyone agrees to a common work language and uses it together can we begin to systematically organize, support, and manage the work. Having a common language also allows people to think in new ways and to build on each other's best thinking.

The questions posed in the previous chapter led the author (Langdon, 1995) to a paradigm for work which he has come to refer to as the "Work Formula." Just as an architect's model represents what a building will eventually be, the Work Formula represents operationally what work is or could be, if we are planning for the future. Thus, the Work Formula serves as the anchor for The Language of Work Model.

Once populated with the data for your particular work at the individual and team (or business or core process) levels, the "work models" (using the Work Formula) show a clear picture that all parties created and can agree to. Once a group agrees upon the data in this Work Formula, that group is in a position to apply it to critical business issues, assuring work alignment, creating transparency, implementing work, and helping to make possible continuous improvements to all aspects of what it takes to be a successful organization.

The Language of Work: Six-Element Work Formula

Back when the author was preparing to be a chemistry teacher, he learned the power of formulas. Chemistry, like any science, is based on predictable results. For example, a formula called Boyle's Law relates volume, pressure, and temperature to one another. The formula states that when you increase the pressure, the volume will predictably change as the temperature remains constant. The user knows that this formula will always produce the same results. It's a little bit more complex, but having and using the Work Formula can produce the same—or at least more highly—predictable results.

The Language of Work employs a Work Formula of six related and systemic elements that define and operationalize work. You could think of it as a "template" for numerous kinds of work. In the same way that anyone can now produce a professional presentation given a PowerPoint template, so too can you now fill in the six-element Work Formula and more fully understand any kind of work—current or future.

To summarize and set the stage for postulating a Work Formula, the six questions concerning what work is in Chapter 1 are reposted in Figure 1, below.

	ELEMENT	QUESTION
Do You Know What Work Is?	**Outputs**	Do you and the team know exactly what deliverables are to be produced?
	Inputs	Can you explicitly identify what will initiate your work and list the resources needed to produce the deliverables?
	Conditions	Do you and the team know what internal rules and/or external regulations impact how you do the work?
	Consequences	Can you state the "value" or impact your deliverables will have for you, customers, and the business as a whole?
	Process Steps	What steps or procedures do you use to achieve the outputs and consequences?
	Feedback	How do you know if mid-course corrections in your work are needed and how do you tell when the work is satisfactorily done?

Figure 1

The same work elements are shown in Figure 2 in the form of a flow diagram. The diagram is important because it depicts the interrelationships of the six elements. What remains is to agree on what these elements mean and their relationship to one another so that we all are thinking of them in the same way.

Put in the context of your own business environment, you could then share meaning with others when defining and deciding how to organize, manage, implement, or change work, minimizing confusion or misunderstanding.

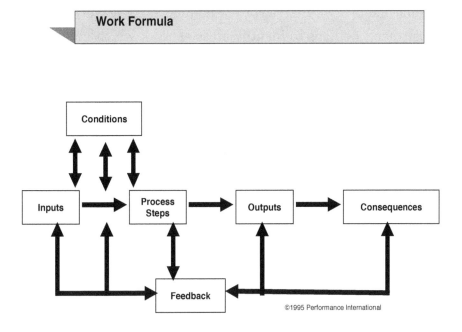

Figure 2

We will now describe how we go about ensuring everyone understands the Work Formula prior to its use in an organization. This may look like a digression, but it is vital to the effective use of the Work Model.

In our work with others, we begin virtually every engagement through an introductory Language of Work tool entitled "The Work Formula: A 10-Minute Teach." It's a short slide show that quickly establishes a shared understanding of what work is. It orients everyone to each of the six work elements using an analogy drawn from American football. A version of the 10-Minute Teach that applies to jobs and work groups is provided below. A full, free version can be found on YouTube at https://youtu.be/Nn7tLm-4nRLU. Feel free to use it.

Imagine that we are ready to begin modeling the work of your department, perhaps to identify areas of work which you might want to improve or change.

The 10-Minute Teach

*"The Language of Work Formula is a way to represent the interrelated elements that comprise work. The Work Formula can be used to define work at various levels and layers of a business. Today we are going to put together your work group (or job) model. As you look at the Work Formula (in Figure 2), each of you will give it your own personal meaning. However, we need to establish and share a **common** meaning for each word. Also, these six elements have a dynamic relation to one another, which we illustrate by the arrows, and the relationships need to be well understood and applied, both individually and collectively. We will look at the definitions first and then at the behavioral relationships.*

*Note that three of the elements—inputs, process steps, and output—are the classic manufacturing model. Henry Ford, for example, understood and applied this model quite effectively in building an entire industry based on producing automobiles. He took various identified resources (**inputs**), utilized them through assembly-line manufacturing (**process steps**) to produce **outputs** (cars). That was all he was concerned with as far as an understanding of work. It was ground-breaking at the time in the definition of work and had significant worldwide consequences.*

But Ford's view of work assumed that the workers were cogs in a machine. Now we know that humans are not robots and need data to perform well. Recognizing that performance is the behavior of people, we have added three additional elements that more fully capture work. These are: consequences, conditions, and feedback. Thus, when outputs are produced, they must result in usable **consequences** *to the business, follow important* **conditions** *that govern the work, and are aided by* **feedback** *(communication) that helps the work be completed correctly and to the satisfaction of clients or customers.*

A sports analogy, American football, will tie these work elements together and give further clarity in their use. In this instance, let's take the work execution of one work group in football—the defense— and model it using the Work Formula. Defense is the work group that tries to keep the other team's offense from scoring. We will illustrate this in a very basic model without the usual details of a real work group model (to be shown later). The defense work group model is shown (in condensed form) in Figure 3 on next page.

When a work group such as this is modeled, we begin by specifying the outputs (listed at the right). This tells us what the group produces as products or services. For example, the defense (work group) tackles, sacks, recovers fumbles, tries to intercept the ball, and so on. It does this to achieve the consequences of countering the efforts of the opposing team's offense. It needs certain inputs from the coaches, other players, the defensive coordinator, and so on. It must follow certain conditions such as the NFL rules, its own defensive playbook, etc. It achieves the

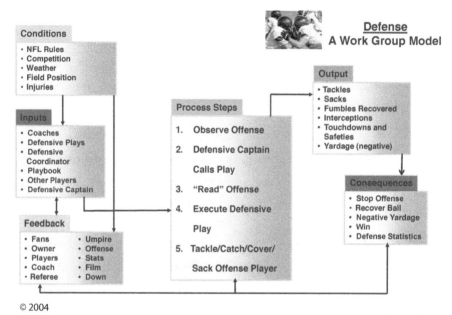

Conditions
- NFL Rules
- Competition
- Weather
- Field Position
- Injuries

Defense
A Work Group Model

Output
- Tackles
- Sacks
- Fumbles Recovered
- Interceptions
- Touchdowns and Safeties
- Yardage (negative)

Inputs
- Coaches
- Defensive Plays
- Defensive Coordinator
- Playbook
- Other Players
- Defensive Captain

Process Steps
1. Observe Offense
2. Defensive Captain Calls Play
3. "Read" Offense
4. Execute Defensive Play
5. Tackle/Catch/Cover/ Sack Offense Player

Consequences
- Stop Offense
- Recover Ball
- Negative Yardage
- Win
- Defense Statistics

Feedback
- Fans
- Owner
- Players
- Coach
- Referee
- Umpire
- Offense
- Stats
- Film
- Down

© 2004

Figure 3

outputs by using prescribed process steps that we have generalized here at a very high level in a five-step sequence—understanding, of course, that more detailed steps could be specified as to how each output is achieved. And the work of the defense is enhanced and encouraged by the use of feedback from such sources as the referees, fans, and other players. Again, greater detail would be provided in an actual work group model.

This just illustrates one level of work in an organization—the work group level. Continuing our analogy, other levels would be the business unit (franchise), the core processes (play of the game, marketing, merchandizing, recruiting, etc.), and jobs (players). In organizing and managing your department, we are concerned with modeling only work groups and jobs. (Note: managers of more than one department will need to also *model core processes as well. This is delineated in* The Business Model *of* The Work Trilogy.*)*

We have seen a work group modeled, so let's look at an individual job. We will define it again at a high level, for illustrative purposes.

Figure 4 illustrates the job model of a quarterback, one of several players on a football team. Using the Work Formula six-element template, we can model the quarterback job in the same way we modeled the work group. Doing this makes clear for the first time the relationship among the team's work groups (defense, offense, and special teams) and the work of various individual job holders. This clarity allows us to align the individual jobs to the work group and vice versa. As you see in Figure 4, you can illustrate the quarterback job in terms of the outputs produced to achieve consequences by using certain inputs, following conditions, process steps, and aided by feedback.

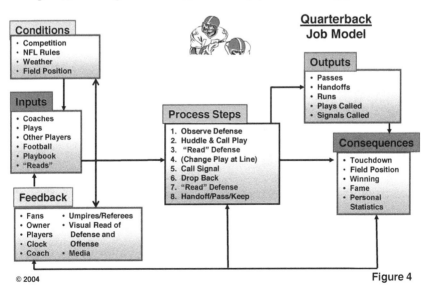

Quarterback Job Model

Conditions
- Competition
- NFL Rules
- Weather
- Field Position

Inputs
- Coaches
- Plays
- Other Players
- Football
- Playbook
- "Reads"

Feedback
- Fans
- Owner
- Players
- Clock
- Coach
- Umpires/Referees
- Visual Read of Defense and Offense
- Media

Process Steps
1. Observe Defense
2. Huddle & Call Play
3. "Read" Defense
4. (Change Play at Line)
5. Call Signal
6. Drop Back
7. "Read" Defense
8. Handoff/Pass/Keep

Outputs
- Passes
- Handoffs
- Runs
- Plays Called
- Signals Called

Consequences
- Touchdown
- Field Position
- Winning
- Fame
- Personal Statistics

© 2004

Figure 4

Figure 5 provides a useful summary of the six elements that comprise the LoW Formula. These elements are listed, defined, and typified in the order in which all levels of work would be best modeled.

The Language of Work Formula

Work Modeling Definition Job Aid

ELEMENT	DEFINITION	TYPICAL SOURCES	TYPES
Output	That which is produced/ provided for stakeholders as tangible deliverables	• Services • Products • Knowledge	
Input	The resources and requests available or needed to produce outputs. What must be present for something (the output) to happen.	• Client Needs • People • Ideas • Equipment • Facilities • Funds • Information • Specific requests	➢ Triggers ➢ Resources
Conditions	Existing factors that influence the use of inputs and processes to produce outputs.	• Rules • Policies • Regulations • Governance	➢ Internal ➢ External
Consequences	The effects that an output has on a person, product, service, or situation.	• Customer Satisfaction • Needs Met • Problem Solved • Opportunity Realized	➢ Company ➢ Stakeholders ➢ Personal ➢ Societal
Process Steps	The steps completed to use the inputs, under the conditions, in order to produce the outputs.	Steps are represented by action verbs such as: • Produce • Review • Edit • etc.	
Feedback	That which completes the work cycle; response to outputs that confirms success or indicates adjustment is needed. Also, response to processing, conditions, and feedback.	• Client Reactions • Information Needs • Reinforcements	➢ During ➢ After

© 1995

Figure 5

(END of 10-Minute Teach)

After the 10-Minute Teach, the facilitator begins to populate the data. She does this by posting answers from the group to the first question, which is "What do you (or your team) produce?" The answers from the group are often wordy; sometimes people need time to discuss the answers because they have never thought of themselves as producing deliverables (outputs). The key skill the facilitator brings at this point is the ability to boil many words into a number that will fit the box on the template. For example, a participant might answer the question "What is one of your deliverables?" by saying:

"I write an assessment by interviewing multiple subjects and conducting focus groups about the conditions in the local jail that are leading to breakouts and riots." The facilitator would make that "Jail Assessments Completed" in the box.

Simultaneously the other facilitator enters the data into an electronic template of boxes and arrows. When that template is projected onto a wall, the group sees in real time how their individual understanding of the work becomes a shared understanding.

This formula for defining work provides a straightforward, objective depiction of work results (outputs and consequences) and describes how the work is executed (inputs, conditions, process steps and feedback) to produce those results. We have found that members of an organization know all these aspects of work, but have not had a template to define and agree on them in a form that is useful for analysis, implementation, and improvement. Thus, the Work Formula provides a common framework for understanding how things are and how they might be made more efficient.

Chapter 4

Work Analytics

Users of the Language of Work Formula have been able to apply it to a variety of business needs. The most frequent application has been in job models—hundreds, perhaps thousands, of jobs have been successfully modeled in this format. Others have used the Language of Work to effectively organize or reorganize their businesses and to solve business problems. Still others use it as an aid to managing more effectively. We have been able to coach clients in new and different applications of the model, and over the years have developed various tools to make it much easier to apply. Several of these are presented here for your use.

> This chapter introduces a set of analytical tools that can be used to develop, implement, and continuously improve work using the Language of Work Formula.

You can use the Work Formula to define a given piece of work, then analyze it, plan its implementation and make improvements in Business Model, Managing Model, and Working Model. These tools are called Work Analytic Tools (WATs) and were created by the authors over years of application in all kinds of businesses. They make applying the Work Formula easy and effective. Relative to *The Working Model* these tools generally take the form of Models, Matrices, AS IS/TO BE Tables, and the Work Formula itself.

Job and Work Group Models

There are two work models especially relevant for job holders: job models and work group models. Two other models (core process and business) of the LoW are primarily for managerial and executive use and need not be detailed here. Each tool is structured using the six elements of the Work Formula, with some additional useful segments especially suited to the Job Model.

The general format for displaying the Work Formula as applied to jobs or work groups is illustrated in the following two figures. It is called a "Work Model":

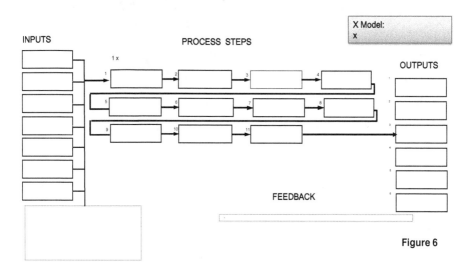

Figure 6

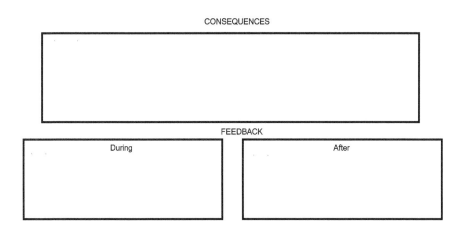

CONSEQUENCES

FEEDBACK

| During | After |

Figure 7

Work models, such as illustrated in Figures 6 and 7, are a specialized LoW version of flowcharting that incorporate all six elements of the Work Formula. The work models not only portray what work is to be achieved and how it is to be done, but also make recognizable the relationship of each work element to the others. This alignment helps achieve overall work efficiency and effectiveness, but most especially can show breakages in the link between the work of individuals and groups. Models may be represented in either a state of AS IS, TO BE, or both. If desired, models may also be used to achieve a level of transparency never before available throughout an organization.

This first WAT—the Job Model and the Work Group Model—when completed, allows you to illuminate your role as an individual and as part of a team. Other useful features, such as skills and knowledge, can be added to amplify the application to work understanding, training, employee selection, and any needed changes. This information is also useful in hiring the right people for jobs, developing orientations, improving work performance on the job, and in developing responses to intended business changes.

Work Matrices

Work matrices are used to display the layers of work that an organization must assure are in place to successfully support work execution. These matrices relate specifically to work standards, work support, human relations, and financial support.

Each matrix employs the Work Formula on one axis and four levels of work execution on the other axis. Thus, it is possible on one hand to show a direct, systemic relationship among the six elements, and the relationship between the six elements and the business unit, core processes, job, and work group levels on the other. A standards matrix (not shown) is specialized to reflect standards in terms of quality, quantity, cost, and timeliness.

Each of the matrices may first be used to decide what work layer support is desired. Later they serve in evaluation on an ongoing basis, helping to determine what work support may need improving. We recommend that you tailor the matrices we provide here to your specific business environment. In this book, we will specifically look at how to use a Work Matrix for assuring adequate Work Support for Work Execution at the job and work group/team levels.

Figure 8 is a sample layout of a Work Support Matrix—minus the specific details within them that we shall introduce in the context of the appropriate work implementation models (found at the end of this book).

WORK SUPPORT MATRIX	INPUT	CONDITIONS	PROCESS	OUTPUT	CONSEQUENCES	FEEDBACK
BUSINESS UNIT	*STRATEGY & BUS. PLANS*	*CULTURE / CONTROLS*	*ADMINISTRATIVE SYSTEMS*	*BUSINESS DELIVERABLES*	*BUSINESS RESULTS*	*BUSINESS MEASUREM./EVALUAT.*
	1A	1B	1C	1D	1E	1F
CORE PROCESSES	*PROCESS RESOURCES*	*REGULATIONS/ POLICIES*	*TECHNOLOGIES (SOFT & HARD)*	*PROCESS DELIVERABLES*	*PROCESS RESULTS*	*CONFIRMATIONS & CORRECTIONS*
	2A	2B	2C	2D	2E	2F
JOBS	*CLIENT NEEDS & RESOURCES*	*WORK INFLUENCES*	*WORK METHODS*	*JOB DELIVERABLES*	*INDIVIDUAL RESULTS*	*CONFIRMATIONS & SELF ADJUSTMENT*
	3A	3B	3C	3D	3E	3F
WORK GROUPS	*CLIENT NEEDS & RESOURCES*	*VALUES & PRACTICES*	*INTERFACE/ RELATIONSHIPS*	*WORK GROUP DELIVERABLES*	*WORK GROUP RESULTS*	*MANAGEMENT/TEAM INFORMATION SYSTEM*
	4A	4B	4C	4D	4E	4F

Figure 8

AS IS/TO BE Models and Tables

The Work Formula provides an excellent scaffolding for doing AS IS (and then) TO BE analysis. In traditional AS IS/TO BE analysis, all the facts (and opinions, perhaps) are gathered and placed in some construct for analysis. By using the Work Formula as the construct, analysis is much less emotional and time consuming.

The first step is to decide whether the focus of the analysis is on work execution (business unit, core processes, jobs, or work groups). If yes, the analysis of a model of the particular level of work should be constructed. That serves as the AS IS model. Then, a facilitated discussion can take place to determine what the TO BE model (again of business unit, etc.) should look like. Will it have some different outputs or consequences? Will inputs be different or arrive in a different form? What changes when it comes to process steps, conditions, and feedback? You will have constructed an AS IS/TO BE Wat using work models.

AS IS/TO BE ANALYSIS   PROJECT: _____

	INPUTS	CONDITIONS	PROCESS STEPS	OUTPUTS	CONSEQUENCES	FEEDBACK
AS IS						
TO BE						

Figure 9

A similar process can be applied to a situation that does not lend itself to modeling. It may be that many facts have been assembled and a solution is needed that has eluded smart people. In this case, classify the various facts, perceptions, etc. in a table using the Work Formula as both an AS IS and TO BE, such as illustrated in Figure 9. One organizes the outputs, consequences, inputs, conditions, process steps, and feedback. By looking at each work element systematically and in relationships to each other, particularly in group analysis, a picture will emerge which all parties agree on. By painting a picture together, seeing it graphically as both AS IS and TO BE, the answers to the issues reveal themselves.

Work Formula

The previously introduced Work Formula (Figure 2), which will be described further in the next chapter, is not only a means for modeling or supporting various levels of work, but is also a way to actualize many of the activities you may engage in, such as planning, reviewing work performance, or improving efficiency or effectiveness. Think, for example, how you might use the six elements of the Work Formula to hold a discussion that reviews your work performance with your manager. What questions might it help you ask?

In the next two chapters we will get into many uses of the Work Formula for these activities.

Now that you have been introduced to some of the most often-used WATs (and there are others) as they relate to the individual and the team, we will explore the ways the WATs can help you see how to effectively and efficiently implement work.

Chapter 5

Work Implementation: Your Job

The world of work is full of surprises—and many aspects of work are complex, as well as challenging. You may have experienced a performance review with low marks for tasks you didn't know were yours to do or heard gossip about incompetence. Or you may have received an email asking for an update on a project you thought was months away. Such surprises are always stress builders, and the LoW can help reduce or eliminate these.

Besides the technical aspects of your work as an individual, how you go about making plans and decisions should be effective and efficient. Here you learn how to use the Work Formula, through various Work Analytic Tools as a systems approach to job implementation.

Many such problems might be attributed to "miscommunication" or poor management—and perhaps that's so. The remedy is to develop and implement Job and Work Group Models individually and with managers, using the various Work Analytic Tools (WATs) to achieve work clarity.

All employees would like to avoid unpleasant surprises. And managers too would prefer not to have to deliver bad news. When the Work Formula is applied to an individual job, it provides new insight into the scope, purpose, impact, governances and relationships vital to that job. Clarity of tasks is provided by the systematic listing of deliverables, their consequences, the inputs needed, the rules that must be followed, the process steps and feedback loops . . . all on just a few pieces of paper.

Once job models exist in an organization, supervisors and employees can clarify roles with others. This is as simple as identifying whose output is input to whom—and how a given output will be input to another person or group. Or perhaps it's a question of who is responsible for given shared steps of a process. A supervisor can also clearly show how the business supports the work by discussing training opportunities, performance review cycles, etc. The Job Model and the Work Group Model clarify bottlenecks, inadequate tools, or unwritten procedures so that solutions become obvious. Discussions about how to make needed changes or continuous improvements, how to work smarter with management facilitation, and other issues are all made possible through operational reflections—models—of one's work.

It is obvious that most businesses have no commonly understood way to view and depict work—a *language of work*—but we have introduced such a Language of Work and will now see in detail how to display and act upon it. For you as an individual, the Job Model—a WAT—will help with many work needs and problems. Other WATs, including the Work Group Model, will be introduced after the Job Model for your use in improving individual and team work.

A Context for Work Implementation

Learning how to use the Work Formula will be easier if the various functions of work implementation that you and others typically perform are organized and shared. In *The Managing Model*, we introduced managers to a picture of their work functions and interactions with workers and teams. This is known to as the Manager/Worker Interface.

The "Manager/Worker Interface," shown in Figure 10, uses a relationship chart to list the various functions that you, as a worker, share (middle column) with your manager. The rest of the chart shows those functions the manager performs (left side) primarily on his/her own, and those for which you, as a worker, are almost exclusively responsible (right side). This will help you envision the many ways both you and management can use the Language of Work in a shared approach that has been difficult until now.

It is no surprise that workers and managers often see the world of work differently. Rarely are their respective functions made clear—instead, lore is passed from one manager to another, one employee to another. Each has a different perspective, so it is no wonder that "alignment" is difficult, if not impossible, and more complex than it need be.

The Worker/Manager Interface demonstrates that shared use of the Work Formula to implement or augment each function makes close alignment possible. This idea of *work alignment* is a central theme throughout the Language of Work. It is much more than a marketing slogan or a catchy idea. Alignment allows employees to work effectively individually and in teams while being managed/

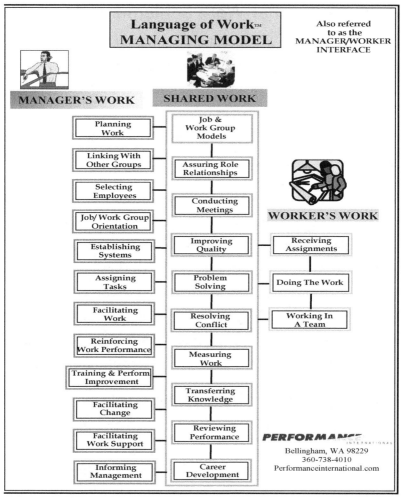

Figure 10

facilitated by managers. It aids employee engagement, reduces turn-over, and makes work life less stressful. Such alignment is primarily achieved by use of a Work Formula identifying the various levels and layers of the Language of Work. But there are also more subtle ways of further assuring alignment, such as that imbedded in use of the Worker/Manager Interface and other features of the Language of Work Model.

Now let's look at how alignment plays out in several practical ways. We begin, naturally, with the Job Model that delineates your work as an individual.

Job Models

In general terms, a Job Model for a Business Analyst, as illustrated in Figures 11-14, is an updated, behaviorally based job description. But, as you will soon learn, such models are much more useful to you and the business.

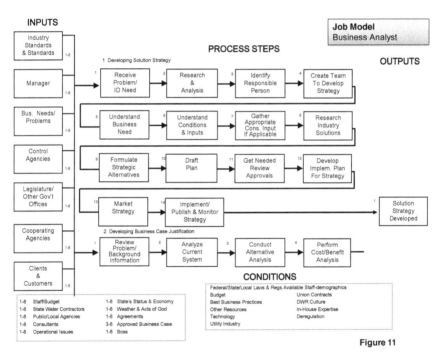

Figure 11

Job Model
Business Analyst

CONSEQUENCES

1. Contributing to viability of Water Resources Agency (outputs 1-8)
2. Integrated system (outputs 1-8)
3. Satisfied customers (outputs 1-8)
4. Cost effectiveness (outputs 1-8)
5. Increased effectiveness and efficiency of IT (outputs 1-8)
6. Changed paradigm (outputs 1-8)
7. Problems solved (outputs 1-8)
8. Informed/skilled users (outputs 3-4)
9. Process improvements (outputs 1-8)
10. Automation of processes (outputs 1-8)
11. Supporting compliance of laws (outputs 1-8)
12. Increased decision support (outputs 1-8)

FEEDBACK

During

1. External Customers
2. System Tools
3. Control Agencies
4. User/Clients
5. Process Owners
6. Executive Management
7. System Performance
8. Vendors
9. Consultants
10. Other Integrated Functional Areas
11. Peers

After

1. Public/Media
2. System Tools
3. Control Agencies
4. User/Clients
5. Process Owners
6. Executive Management
7. System Performance
8. Vendors
9. Consultants
10. Peers
11. External Customers

Figure 12

SKILLS AND KNOWLEDGE

Job Model
Business Analyst

PROCESS

Process for Output 1: Solution Strategy
Skills
- Analytic skills
- Strategic Development
- Planning
- Marketing
Knowledge
- Policies
- Control Agencies
- Public Needs
- IT Industry
- Networking with Peers & Mentors
- Organization Knowledge
- Organization Savvy
- Organization Culture
- Budgeting
- Best Practices
- Business Discipline
- Agency Mission, Goals, Objectives

Process for Output # 2: Business Case Justification
Skills
- Math
- Project Management
- IT Tools/Systems
- Budget
Knowledge
- Applications Limitations
- Agency IT Methodologies

Process for Output # 3: Expertise & Advice
Skills
- Communication: Oral, Written, Verbal, Listening
- Consulting
Knowledge
- Business Disciplines
- Agency Business Processes

Process for Output # 4: Training
Skills
- Training Methods
- Instructional Development
- Analysis
- Evaluation
- Writing
Knowledge
- Business Content

Process for Output # 5: Functional Specifications
Skills
- Research
- Graphics Design
Knowledge
- Application Limitations
- Agency IT Methodologies

Process for Output # 6: Applications/Interfaces/Transactions
Skills
- Analytic
- Writing
- Presentation/Training
- Communication: Interpersonal, Oral, Written

Figure 13

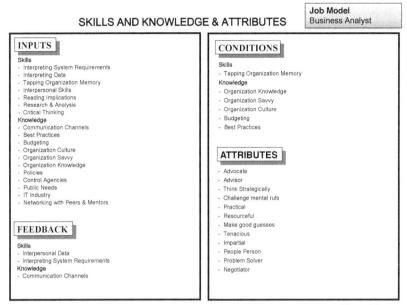

SKILLS AND KNOWLEDGE & ATTRIBUTES

Job Model
Business Analyst

INPUTS

Skills
- Interpreting System Requirements
- Interpreting Data
- Tapping Organization Memory
- Interpersonal Skills
- Reading Implications
- Research & Analysis
- Critical Thinking

Knowledge
- Communication Channels
- Best Practices
- Budgeting
- Organization Culture
- Organization Savvy
- Organization Knowledge
- Policies
- Control Agencies
- Public Needs
- IT Industry
- Networking with Peers & Mentors

FEEDBACK

Skills
- Interpersonal Data
- Interpreting System Requirements

Knowledge
- Communication Channels

CONDITIONS

Skills
- Tapping Organization Memory

Knowledge
- Organization Knowledge
- Organization Savvy
- Organization Culture
- Budgeting
- Best Practices

ATTRIBUTES

- Advocate
- Advisor
- Think Strategically
- Challenge mental ruts
- Practical
- Resourceful
- Make good guesses
- Tenacious
- Impartial
- People Person
- Problem Solver
- Negotiator

Figure 14

One of the more significant problems with traditional job descriptions is that they generally describe principally the outcomes of work, usually in the form of accountabilities, responsibilities, and perhaps "competencies." These features, as you have already surmised, are useful, but only cover a sixth to a third of what constitutes the complete definition of a job. While often good at describing individual work, job descriptions are not of practical use in implementing and improving work. This is true even when work examples, dimensions, and desired attributes are added to job descriptions. Furthermore, job descriptions are often "puffed-up" to make the job holder appear more critical and therefore, more able to justify higher compensation.

In examining hundreds of traditional job descriptions, we have found that the first 25-40% of each are usually job-performance-related. Then the writers start dreaming—that is, they create a wish-list of attributes and characteristics they hope the job holder would have. These are often factors that have little to do with actual work. Job models, on the other hand, are operational depictions of the work, with supporting details in the way of desired entry-level behavior, skills, knowledge, and attributes needed to support the execution of the work. In addition, the specifications of work behavior found in a Job Model can be used as the basis for current work assignments, future changes, performance evaluation, making improvements in skills and efficiency, and can be useful in career development—all of which will be described here in terms of how the Work Formula can be used to implement each of them.

If your management has employed *The Business Model* or *The Managing Model* of the *Work Trilogy*—the Language of Work—you have most likely been exposed to a Job Model. You either directly participated as one of the exemplary job performers in modeling your job, or perhaps you reviewed or helped validate what the job modeling team developed. If you have not yet had your job modeled, you will want to get it done as soon as feasible. This can be accomplished by modeling the job on your own, doing it with your manager or with others in your department, or perhaps working with a skilled facilitator certified in job modeling.

If you have an existing Job Model, as represented by the sample, then you know that a job model is based on the six elements of the Work Formula. Because job descriptions are used in Human Resources departments for hiring, additional elements are usually specified: skills/knowledge, desired job attributes, minimum requirements, responsibilities/accountabilities, competencies, and such.

The Job Model provides clarity beyond what one typically knows about individual work. It is an operational specification of what you are to produce (outputs) to achieve results (consequences), initiated by inputs as triggers and resources, adhering to certain conditions, completed through process steps, and aided by various forms of communication (feedback). Compared to job descriptions that mainly specify only results (e.g., responsibilities/accountabilities), the operational nature of the Job Model provides far more clarity.

Let's break this down to see what is explicit in the behavioral content and use of the Job Model:

Your individual Job Model is first and foremost an *operational representation* of your work as prescribed by the business. While it doesn't have all the minute details in a technical sense, there is enough that both you and others—particularly your manager—have a clear definition of your role in the organization.

Some organizations have tried to use detailed process maps as operational job descriptions. These have proved, consistently, to be of little value, because the brain can only handle five to seven thoughts at a time. A LoW job model maintains a higher level of granularity, which then allows you and your team or manager to fill in details in an organized, systemic, and systematic way.

Having articulated the six elements of work in behavioral/performance terms (as illustrated in Figures 11-12), it is then possible to specify the skills and knowledge (as illustrated in Figures 13-14) needed to technically perform the job. Gone are the wish lists and fantasies. Instead, the attributes, competencies, and skills needed are linked to the execution of the job. Job models are developed by people who know the job intimately—usually exemplary performers or other experts. Gone are the newly minted wage and salary specialists who try, through interviewing content experts, to develop a job description in a mold useful primarily for grading the job and assigning salary levels.

By the way, we are often asked how the Human Resources department reacts to the introduction of a tool that seems to be in their bailiwick. We have had great success in working with HR departments by showing them how to use the Job Model as an input device for HR needs. It is quite easy to convert the Job Model into a traditional job description, because the outputs and consequences together make up the "accountabilities" required in most job description templates.

With the basics of what constitutes the Job Model, let us learn to use it and other analytic tools to implement various aspects of your work as listed in the Worker/Manager Interface.

Work Implementation Roles
for the Job Holder

As previously noted, various work functions are illustrated in the Worker/Manager Interface (Figure 10)—see page 44. By way of indicating the congruence of the books in this trilogy, this figure duplicates Figure 25 of *The Managing Model*, the second eBook in the *Work Trilogy*. There are over 25 listed implementation roles for the manager, between manager and worker, and for workers. Let us describe each role that you, as an individual or working in combination with your manager, can better perform using the Work Formula and other Work Analytic Tools (WATs).

We begin with the often needed–and often ignored—orientation to your role.

Job Orientation
Job Model

Managers traditionally are expected to conduct job orientation. However, we know of more than one occasion where managers were too busy—or perhaps too cavalier, or just not a communicative type—to orient a new employee. One engineer told us he sat next to the department secretary's desk for two weeks—doing nothing—as his orientation. Perhaps his manager thought osmosis would work! Using a Job Model to orient a new employee to the job is simple and requires little or no preparation. First the manager could talk about the outputs (deliverables). This is where expectations can be made clear—and "flavor" (that is, the unwritten expectations) can be made clear as well. Then go on to describe the inputs needed and where they can be obtained; provide samples of deliverables; discuss the consequences (the all-important "why" of the job and its impact on others); assemble the documents that contain the conditions; and provide any job aids, checklists, or procedure manuals for the process steps. And be sure to introduce the new person to others, giving a little intel on why the person was selected or an interest or skill that will help build the team.

If your new manager is not ready to orient you, you could orient yourself by using a Job Model to observe how your department operates. Or sitting with your job model in hand in the presence of another worker as a holder of that job. What are the job deliverables? Its inputs? How does the process compare with your training in the field? What are the consequences to the organization of this department's running well? What are the governances that it follows? You might be able to observe a lack of feedback, given your treatment as a new employee. After making these observations, you can then ask for procedures manuals to identify process steps as well (we would hope) as conditions (governances). If you use the Job Model systematically and well, you can not only get a handle on your own job, but you may boost—and be seen to boost—your value to the company.

One of the more unsettling aspects of any job is the need to orient us to job changes. Changes in equipment, technology, modernization, reorganization, or mergers all create uncertainty. Uncertainty is that visceral feeling of not knowing how the future will be different. Virtually all jobs have changes; some seem to occur even daily. These are more than typical thoughts in the face of change:

"Exactly what part of my job will be changing?"

"Will I end up doing more--or less of this . . . or that?"

"What will happen to that information I used to collect?"

"Is my work less important now?"

We suggest that you and your manager use your Job Model to discuss what will change long before the change itself is scheduled to take place.

Using the previously introduced Business Analyst Job Model (figure 11) as an example, let us say that the legislature is planning

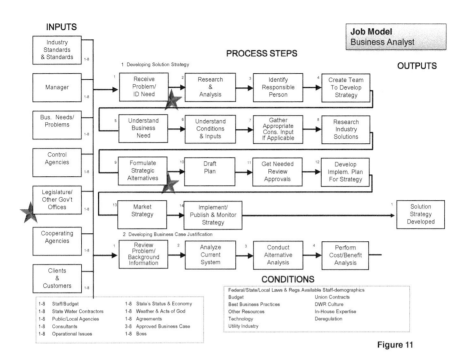

Figure 11

to make a change that will affect this job. By focusing on the Job Model the uncertainty around how this change will affect the people in this position can be reduced. The ★ in the input at the left shows the source of the change. Then a review of the process steps shows that only two of the process steps will be affected. In this scenario, maybe the legislature is intending to limit the amount of information that will be available to the public; if passed this will affect the problems that will be given to the business analyst as well as the strategies that person will need to develop in order to provide the deliverable, "Solution Strategy Delivered." Here are some of the questions that should be asked, using the Job Model to reduce uncertainty in the face of change.

Will outputs and/or consequences change?

Are there new or changing conditions to follow?

What inputs will change?

What specific steps of the processes will be affected?

Will feedback change?

Will new skills and knowledge be needed?

We have seen people skip the normal grieving and denial stages after major changes—even layoffs—by thinking clearly about the work they used to do and the work they will do in the future. It helps to be dispassionate about the changes . . . to see them clearly. When the changes are visible in black and white you can be prepared to deal with them.

In a Job Model, you are not seeking to know or master the changes, but rather to get an overall sense of them—so that you know what to expect. Once this is achieved, you can more readily assess the impact the change might have on your normal duties, allowing you to look at "the new normal" in a systematic, nonthreatening way. Associated factors can be noted as well. A discussion of a new Job Model in comparison with the present one is far more concrete, less emotion-driven, more public, and more helpful in the success of the projected change.

Assigning Tasks
Job Models

From the manager's point of view, giving assignments is a matter of telling the worker(s) what to do. From the worker's point of view, task assignment is more about, "What is he saying?" or "How am I going to do that?"

We are not suggesting that you literally have your Job Model in front of you every time a task is assigned, but it is clearer and more effective if both you and the manager are seeing task assignments from the same point of view. First, every Job Model has "boss" or "manager" as an input. So the input (boss) tells you what deliverable (output or product) is expected. By providing the consequences (or impact—or even the reason for the task), the manager helps place the assignment in context.

Thinking and acting this systematically is helpful to both of you. The manager usually has many thoughts going on: others to meet with, her boss to respond to, his own deliverables to produce. The employee is focused on the need for information in order to proceed. When the employee's questions are clear and to the point (What process steps should I use? What conditions apply? What feedback loop will be useful to assure accurate completion? … are just some to be asked) managers are able to be more efficient and effective in their communication. The potential impact on other aspects of the job, such as priorities, time, resources, and other expectations can be discussed. That's one of the values of having a common LoW. It makes the manager confident that the employee understands the assignment.

If your manager has not yet caught up with your use of the Work Formula and Job Model as job/role or task tool, then whenever a task assignment is given, you should immediately begin to ask yourself (and the manager, as needed), any necessary questions on the task input, conditions that govern it, the process steps you will be utilizing (and with whom, as another input), and feedback that will help you along the way, as well as knowing when you have successfully completed the task assignment.

In our own business we were adding a family member to our group. She had many new skills and perspectives, and we were excited about bringing her on. Each time we had a meeting, one or the other of us would "dump" a bunch of ideas, contacts, and perspectives on her. It didn't take very long for us to realize that we had to focus on certain deliverables (such as "build a website" or "expand networking opportunities") as specific assignments that we could all focus on, using—imagine!—the Language of Work.

Informing Management
 Work Formula

Informing management is expected of most employees. But, often, keeping management informed is seen by a worker as, "I answer your questions when you ask." Managers, on the other hand, hate surprises. They are often angry if an unexpected problem is revealed, especially publicly. Workers no doubt see their approach as a form of damage control; they hope to solve the problem before it catches management's attention.

Make sure your manager understands what particular part(s) of work you want to inform them about. Remember too that managers are very human and have many details in their heads; they appreciate brevity, clarity, and lack of emotionality. Using the Work Formula as a guide, here are some guidelines for providing information to management.

What specific outputs and consequences are you informing the manager about?

- Once you have identified the information that management should have, tell the manager the specific output and its related consequence(s) taken directly from your Job or Work Group Model.
- EX from the Business Analyst Job Model: *"I need to chat a bit about the Solution Strategies I am working on."*

What work conditions, such as rules or regulations, need clarification that would make doing the work easier?

- Tell the manager work conditions that are getting in the way of doing the work.
- EX from the Business Analyst Job Model: *"I'm having some trouble getting the purpose behind the changes in legislation. I read the legislative reports, but don't know what problem they are trying to solve. So I am having trouble thinking of strategies to solve this."*

What difficulties are you having with certain inputs or triggers that initiate work? Are there people in other areas or other departments who want to keep some inputs "secret"?

- Tell the manager what input(s) is/are missing, need to be improved, added, or is/are getting in the way.
- EX from the Business Analyst Job Model: *"Sometimes I think the Government Relations people think I am a spy or something."*

What specific process steps are so unclear that you want further help in learning or practicing with others?

- Tell the manager what process steps are giving you and others difficulty and ask what can be done to make things better.

- EX from the Business Analyst Job Model: *"Given this pending regulation change, how do you think our alternatives will change?"*

Is there more specific feedback or help you'd like to receive while you are doing the work?

- Tell the manager what feedback would help you understand or perform the work better as you go and what feedback you need after work is completed.
- EX from the Business Analyst Job Model: *"Since this is new, can I book a time to review an early draft of my solution strategy—and get your feedback on it?"*

Such specific directions as these make for clearer communication on the six elements that constitute work execution, help keep the discussion on target, and lend themselves to efficient description of the problem. Following these guidelines will mean that there is context for discussion; neither party has to wonder what the other is referring to or make assumptions which may turn out to be incorrect, delaying a potential solution to the issue.

This is just as important when you are talking about work standards, work support, work relations, or financial support. Reference these layers of work so you and the manager are on the same page, using the LoW as a point of common understanding and reaching consensus.

By the way, there is much about informing management that falls squarely on the manager him or herself. A manager seeking information needs to know precisely what he needs to know (as obvious as it may seem). In *The Managing Model* we deal with how the manager can seek and obtain specific information. But a worker can proactively assure an informed management as well. It is relatively simple.

The authors recently worked with the executive director of a nonprofit who was planning a fundraising event. Her reports to the organization's Board of Directors tended to wander, touching first on areas of excitement and then on areas of anxiety, leaving the Board members confused as to progress as well as their own assignments. By developing a Job Model with fundraising events as one of the executive director's deliverables, we were able to reduce anxiety tremendously and enhance the potential success of the event. Clients who have learned the Language of Work have found that it transfers well into their non-work lives in the same way. Cricket teams and Little League baseball teams have been better coached and managed using the Work Formula—even without Job Models. If you are a reader whose organization has not yet adopted the LoW, know that applying it to various other organizations can be very useful—and a good way for you to become adept at it.

Transferring Knowledge
 Job Model

You are likely to need to transfer knowledge about some element of your job. It could be because you are going on vacation, or have a short-term health problem. You may be promoted or for other reasons asked to train a new employee. There are additional reasons for knowledge transfer, including your retirement, change of job, or a merger or acquisition that changes who does your work. Knowledge transfer has become crucial to maintaining business success due to turnover or reorganization. Organizations with aging work forces find the need to transfer knowledge a strategic issue. Models can play a key role in knowledge transfer. We would like to suggest two ways to accomplish this, using a Job Model.

First, the Job Model serves as an orientation tool, as has already been noted. It provides the big picture of the work. By starting with the deliverables and the consequences, you can explain to another person the "what" and the "why" of the job. You can avoid making random observations about the work, including your favorite gripes, war stories, or the truncated bits and pieces that are commonly referred to as the "fire hose" approach—and no one can drink from a fire hose! Instead, after providing the big picture, you can focus on the next two critical elements: the inputs and the conditions. Here, you can tell where to find the various inputs, make observations about the timeliness of receipt, discuss the dynamics of the white space between departments, address triggers and in general flesh out the picture. By covering the conditions, you can save the other person embarrassment and even punishment. (Things that seem logical can be against the law—so Employee Handbooks and HR rules are really helpful, especially to new supervisors. And the unwritten rules that govern culture can be landmines for those new to the organization.) Feedback sources are useful for an employee with new responsibility as well.

Once you have made someone with a new job aware of these elements, he or she can learn the process steps. Often there is more detail in these steps than a person can absorb easily, but by providing any job aids, checklists, worksheets, sample work, historical resources—and linking them to the precise processes for which they are used—you can offer a long-lasting aid to the person you are helping integrate into a new place in the organization.

We have seen clients use numbers under each of the process steps, each number indicating the name or location of a particular resource. When the Skills and Knowledge have been listed, they can serve as a handy checklist of skills possessed and skills needed. This can, in turn, create an effective employee development plan.

There are also important considerations specified in a Job Model in the work standards as you see them, available work support resources, important human relations considerations, financial sources, and so on.

This systematic approach allows the learner to record a great deal of information in a first interview, pursue resources on her own and return—perhaps a week later—to dive deeper.

A second way to transfer knowledge is by of recording with the present or former job holder the nature and scope of the job. A recorded interview focused on the backdrop of the Job Model allows the individual to describe and illustrate how the work was/ is done. Thus, they fill in this template:

> "I typically go about my work as follows, working with these people, using these resources, and often aided by some special ways I figured out for doing the job most effectively with and for others."

Individuals may have devised special forms and tools to aid them in doing their work over the years, and these need to be captured as knowledge to be passed on to others now and in the future.

The alternative is usually a data dump, which is rarely useful to anyone. In addition, people who have been on the job for decades have become unconsciously competent, meaning they may not remember that there was a time when they didn't know what they do now. For a novice, this can be very frustrating. A Job Model allows knowledge to be transferred in a systematic way, and it may keep turnover confusion to a minimum.

Reviewing Performance
 Work Formula

Everybody seems to hate performance reviews! Managers may feel they don't do them well. They see them as a time-consuming, futile exercise, handed down by HR, which puts them in an awkward position with their employees. Few of us want to judge, lest we be judged, unless of course, a manager has sadistic tendencies, wanting to punish and play "gotcha" at least once a year. Such reviews benefit no one.

Employees often hate reviews, too. Again, no one likes to be judged. And most performance reviews don't provide the kind of tangible feedback that can be used to improve actual job performance.

Everyone (managers, employees and HR staff) is so mystified by the process that organizations often try to doctor the review process by making it different. They substitute long forms to give reviewers something structured to fill out; they try to separate performance reviews from compensation; finally, they try to engage everyone possible in the process by requiring 360^0 reviewing as if performance were a popularity contest. Given such, enterprises often abandon the practice. The problem is not that the idea of performance reviews (appraisal, assessment, etc.) is bad, but rather that no one knows exactly what to review. There is, once again, a fundamental lack of understanding about what performance (that is, work) is and how people should talk about it.

Most methods in common use will not succeed. Performance reviews are not an exercise in filling out forms or exercising stern managerial authority, but rather should be a simple discussion about the work one has done, what was well done, and what needs improving over the next year.

In the Language of Work, performance review is viewed in an *effect* and *cause* relationship. Periodically—at least twice a year and preferably on an ongoing basis—the manager needs to review the "effects" a worker is achieving. Using a Job Model to guide a performance review, the manager and worker, as illustrated in Figure 15, first review the outputs and consequences—the combined *effect*—of work. If either output and/or consequences are not being achieved, there is likely a set of *causes* that led to this. These causes are rooted in the other, articulated elements of the work that comprise the Language of Work. Thus, the manager and employee can review—as a beginning point—the inputs, conditions, process steps and/or feedback to identify the root cause of any performance misfire.

The following summarizes some of these root causes for failure to achieve outputs and consequences:

- Were the process steps not followed? Were they not completed? Or were they done poorly?

In behavioral terms, work is a cause and effect relationship. Thus:

CAUSE

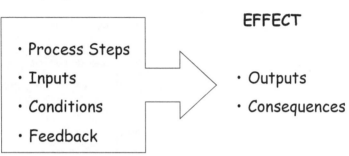

EFFECT

• Process Steps

• Inputs   • Outputs

• Conditions   • Consequences

• Feedback

Figure 15

- Were there inputs from others that were not utilized, came late, or were of poor quality?
- Were there conditions not followed? Or did the conditions serve as obstacles to completing the work?
- Was feedback missing that might have helped make corrections before they went wrong? Or was reinforcement missing?
- Did the organization fail to provide appropriate or needed work support? (Examples: a clear assignment, or a poorly designed work space or lighting.)
- Were underlying skill, knowledge, or attributes lacking?

As the manager and worker analyze the causes of less than ideal outputs or consequences, they emphasize desired work achievement; discuss what worked well and what needs fixing. The question is not one of placing blame, but how whatever fell short could be done better in the future. Since the Job Model provides skills and knowledge specifically related to inputs, conditions, process steps, and feedback, these areas for improvement can be identified in fundamental ways that can lead to enhanced performance.

The results of any such discussion can then be given to Human Resources, so that they can develop remediation strategies and resources across the organization in the form of organization-wide solutions, such as training.

Perhaps the strongest advantage of this approach is that the two parties work together to achieve a common goal: great performance. The Language of Work system helps to keep the conversation nonjudgmental and focused not on personalities, but on elements of work.

Career Development and Career Resilience

 Job Models

Many workers expect to do work that is more interesting, challenging and/or lucrative than what they are currently doing. We recognize that working a lifetime in any single job may be fulfilling for some, but others will leave if they cannot grow within an organization. Organizations miss out when they do not nurture the dreams and expectations of the employees they already have.

The consequences are not just lack of employee engagement, or low morale; there are substantial costs involved in recruiting and training new employees. A strong commitment to career development often minimizes turnover.

At the same time, we must recognize that organizations may not have the brilliance—or the resources—to develop robust talent management or career development programs. And those that are developed might be designed for "high pots" (high-potential employees) or executives-in-training or other groups deemed critical by the enterprise, rather than recognizing that all levels of workers need them.

However, when job models are visible to all, career development is an easy process. Individuals can identify jobs they are interested in, review the requirements clearly delineated in these models, and negotiate terms for learning, practicing, and achieving. This process serves as a self-selection tool: a person can eliminate jobs with outputs or requirements too difficult to achieve or uninteresting to pursue.

By homing in on desirable, achievable jobs, employees can select the ones they are interested in and establish mentoring relationships with holders of those jobs to learn new skills. For example, a junior accountant can establish an agreement with a senior accountant to learn the complexities of a given outputs. A mentoring arrangement can be established between the two parties. The role of a manager is to encourage, support, and assure resources, time and any direct assistance (i.e., job/task shadowing) for their joint effort. This becomes an informal career development opportunity. With thought, it can also provide cross-job training that could prove vital in times of increasing job demands, changes, absences, and the like.

For example, one of the authors realized that work in a similar but different department was intriguing: transactional (day-to-day)

HR instead of strategic (planning) HR. It was a tool she needed to put into her quiver if she was to be selectable for an HR Director job. She identified one of the outputs from the Job Model (employees hired) and requested that her director give her one week of job shadowing. Once she had been successful in this endeavor, she went on to participate in a compensation review, and she was eventually given full transactional HR responsibility for a small department.

One can easily see that a Job Model can make career development more worker-initiated, thus more likely to occur and be satisfactory when actively supported by management. When linked to a career path system supported and established by management and HR, job models play an even greater role.

The process of self-developed career planning is relatively simple, even in situations where numerous job models do not exist. First, model your own current job. Then identify the skills and knowledge needed to perform that job. This describes the AS IS state of your own job. Then model, as best you are able, the job you would like to hold. This tends to be more difficult, because you lack the intimate knowledge you have about your own job. But it is possible to approach a person who holds the job you are interested in. But even without a discussion, it is possible to look at the deliverables (outputs) that the desired job produces. Once you think you have the main ones, you can check with a person holding that job. Add the additional ones you may learn about. Then consider the consequences, conditions, and inputs. Look at the steps that seem to be required to complete each of the deliverables. Again, asking pertinent useful questions can fill in blanks. Finally draft what you see as the skills and knowledge required for that job. Now compare the list from your current job with those listed in the desired job. Highlight the ones that are missing. Determine whether schooling/training is needed, or if any individual skill can be learned through a book or on the job. If the former, seek a way to get the needed courses. If the latter, get the book needed and/or ask for help to job shadow. Look at the deliverables and see what portion of them you can already do. Then negotiate to be able to complete other deliverables, until you have achieved some competence. You will be on your way.

Chapter 6

Work Implementation: Your Role as a Team Player

It might seem at times that we are an island in a sea of workers. But actually we are an important part of the sea; indeed, we are part of an ocean of work that should be aligned with and in harmony with all others.

> In addition to an individual knowing their job well, the Work Formula helps everyone to understand roles in a team. Such alignment makes it much easier to work together.

That "ocean" is the subject of *The Business Model*, a part of *The Work Trilogy*. You might want to review that model at some time. Right now, we will focus on the work you do as part of a team.

A team can benefit in many ways from the development of a Work Group Model, using the LoW system. The alternative to that is to discuss work the same way you have always discussed work; unfortunately, if the results of such a discussion have been unsatisfactory in the past, the likelihood is that they will remain unsatisfactory.

Identifying your role in a team and clarifying and improving that role uses many of the same Work Analytic Tools as you used for your individual job. You won't have to learn anything new to model your team, but you will need the cooperation of others. That cooperation may prove difficult to get, but with a little coaxing, you may be able to show others the numerous benefits they will receive (among which reduction in drama and elimination of confusion are just two) by using the Work Formula to define group work, its execution, and how to improve it. Here, for example, in Figures 16 and 17 is a typical Work Group Model:

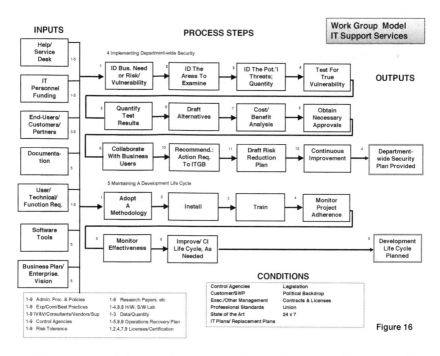

Figure 16

You can model a work group such as this yourself and confirm the model with others. However, it is far better to involve representatives of the various jobs that comprise your work group. The best representatives we often refer to as "exemplary performers"—the

**Work Group Model
IT Support Services**

CONSEQUENCES

1. Increased efficiency (outputs 1-9)
2. Customer satisfaction (outputs 1-9)
3. Cost/appropriate (Balanced Score Card) (outputs 1-9)
4. Stability and consistency of department-wide processes (outputs 1-9)
5. Standardization (outputs 1-9)
6. Trust of process and output (outputs 1-9)
7. Acceptance of expertise (outputs 1-9)
8. Happier employees (outputs 1-4,6,8)
9. Improved/informed decision making (outputs 2, 6-9)
10. Accountability by all parties (outputs 1,2,4,5,7,8)
11. Improved resource management (outputs 1-9)
12. Support the accomplishment of DWR Mission & Vision (outputs 1-9)
13. Appropriate security of IT environment (outputs 2-4,6,8,9)

FEEDBACK

During
1. Client
2. Management
3. IT Governance
4. Performance Monitoring SW
5. Peers
6. Vendors
7. Professional Societies

After
1. Client
2. Management
3. IT Governance
4. Control Agencies
5. Audit
6. Security Performance
7. Performance Monitoring SW
8. Peers
9. Vendors
10. Professional Societies

Figure 17

best of the best. Generally everyone knows who these individuals are. It's also obvious to have the manager involved, since she or he is the head of that team, work group, or department. Everyone, once assembled for about a four-hour work group modeling session, should have read the *Work Formula . . . A 10-Minute Teach or* heard (https://youtu.be/Nn7tLm4nRLU) it. This shared knowledge of what constitutes work is critical for everyone: Everyone needs to be speaking, defining, and using a common view of work to achieve an accurate Work Group Model.

In Figure 16 you see the specification of four of the six elements of a Work Group Model:
- Outputs (on the right)
- Inputs (on the left)

- Conditions (at the bottom), and
- Process Steps (in the middle)

In Figure 17 you find the Consequences and Feedback, the remaining two elements of the Work Group Model.

Most work groups have five to seven major outputs. These are the products or services the group provides/delivers to its internal or external customers/clients. Our sample work group, the IT Support Services Work Group, produces nine services (outputs) as listed below. We'll show only two outputs (those in bold type, below) for illustrative purposes. You find these two outputs on the right side of the work group model in Figure 16.

- Problems solved
- Operations recovery planned
- Data Center services provided
- **Department-wide security provided**
- **Developmental life cycle planned**
- Research/advisory consulting provided
- IT assets managed
- Data managed
- IT audits conducted

Looking further at Figure 16, you see that in order to produce these outputs, the group will need certain inputs—both the triggers that initiate the work, and the resources for producing the outputs. The Help Desk, for example, is a typical trigger input, while Software Tools is a typical resource input.

At the bottom of Figure 16 you will find an extensive list of rules and regulations, the conditions (governances) that the group must be aware of and follow in doing their work. Contracts & Licenses, for example, are one kind of condition.

Next you find two sets of process steps, one each for the two outputs illustrated. One output has a twelve-step process and the other has six steps.

Figure 17 lists first the positive consequences that are to be achieved by the sample department. Each statement is a value outcome to be attained as a result of a set of outputs that should result in the consequence. For example, the first consequence, "Increased efficiency," is the result of all department outputs, while consequence 13, "Appropriate security of IT environment," is the result of outputs 2-4, 6, and 8-9.

Taken together, this Work Group Model is a graphic representation of how the work will be executed. It establishes alignment, consensus and commitment to the features of the work as it relates to overarching core processes of the business. In the future, it becomes the basis upon which change can be planned and aligned. It also represents, of course, your role as it relates to your Job Model, and the basis for the group manager to help facilitate group work. It is critical for you to note that all the elements of both the Work Group and Job Model must be consistent with one another, thus assuring work alignment. In other words, work alignment means that the manager, the members of the group, and you will all look at individual elements of work in exactly the same way, rather than coming at each element from a different background or foundation.

Model Your Work Group Now

If feasible and practical, you might want to model your work group now. Having both the Job and Work Group Models in hand will help you recognize the full value of using the Language of Work to understand, implement, and improve work, as well as to better communicate with others about the work.

Work Implementation Roles for the Team

As previously noted on *The Worker/Manager Interface* (page 44), there are numerous needs for work implementation that you will perform with others as part of a team. The LoW will be helpful in many ways to more effectively fulfill these work implementation needs. We will now describe how various Work Analytic Tools are used to assist in work implementation as a team:

Planning Work
 Work Plan

Planning work, such as for a project, need not be a confusing or random "thing to be accomplished," as is often the practice. We all know planning is about finding effective and efficient ways to go about accomplishing a task or achieving a goal. Thus, like our own work, planning can be approached in a systematic manner. Using a Work Analytical Tool based on the Work Formula, especially with others, provides a functional systems approach to planning work.

Planning work has four phases. The first is deciding what needs to be accomplished for what purpose, and then how. The second phase is deciding who will be involved and at what point in the process. The third is allocating resources. And the fourth is measuring success.

To use the Work Formula for phase 1, you need to specify the intended consequences to be achieved. This usually requires communication and clarification with management on their expectations. Having achieved consensus on outcomes, then decide what outputs will best achieve the stated consequence(s). From these two (consequences and outputs), the work can then be planned (modeled, flowcharted, check listed, etc.) in terms of needed inputs, conditions, process steps, and feedback.

This *pre-work*, if you will, serves to clarify, unify, and resolve many of the questions in the team's collective approach. Once completed in terms of the Work Formula, the pre-work serves as the input to the simple *who, what, when* chart that serves as the basis for all work planning. More elaborate details can be added as needed. Additional resources can be easily identified and allocated or negotiated to complete such a plan. Finally, as the work plan is executed, measuring for success can be monitored against this well-thought-out plan using the Language of Work for effect (outputs and consequences) and cause (inputs, conditions, process steps, and feedback). Finally, in doing the work planning, any needed work standards, work support, human relations, and financial considerations can be identified.

So whether the project is a wedding, a training event, or the installation of enterprise-wide software—or any other project—this work planning process relieves stress, increases cooperation and collaboration, prevents surprises and allows the team to be successful.

Linking with Others

 Work Group and/or Core Process Models

Linking with others, in this context, means your group's relationship with other work groups, rather than with role relationships within your work group.

As a worker, you are usually a part of a honeycomb of interrelated work between members of your department and other groups. Members of the marketing group interact with production and sales. The training group interacts with its clients. Distribution interacts with production; IT, HR, accounting and other staff groups interact with all line groups.

When the inputs your department receives—outputs from another group—are late, for example, your department's work is negatively affected. Then, when your department's output does not meet standards or specifications, the next department's work is affected in terms of timeliness, quality, cost, and perhaps quantity. The linkages between work groups need to be clear to prevent one unit from delaying another or having effects on another's work. Showing the linkages clearly, so that everyone understands the cause-and-effect relationship they have with each other, is critical to the success of the enterprise.

Using the various forms (work levels) of Language of Work Models as the basis for linking work with others, we have found, consistently changes the tone of the work-sharing discussion. When models of core processes or work groups are shared between managers and workers, this discussion can be centered objectively on specific elements of the work, rather than on the generalities of work relationships and issues. This is critical to reaching effective solutions. While other resources (see especially Langdon et al., 2014, on defining core processes as a precursor to identifying jobs) show how this can be done, here we will concern ourselves with making clear the relationships you have with those in your work group and parallel jobs in other work groups.

When your work group and other groups have been modeled using the LoW, you are in a position to see the linkages among them. You will see how your outputs become others' inputs, and their outputs become your inputs. You'll perhaps share common consequences even though you are producing fundamentally different outputs. Or you'll clearly discern the steps you share in a process. For example, we worked with a market research firm whose researchers polled movie theaters on Wednesdays and Thursdays. They approached moviegoers about their reaction to various ads. They asked questions like, "Would you see this movie based on this ad?"

This raw data was turned over to data analyzers who compared answers by demographic group—age, gender, socioeconomic status, sources of information, etc. The analyzers then wrote reports for the client, who would make decisions about the marketing strategy for each movie based on the analysis.

So the first group's output was "data collected." This served as input to the data analyzers. Their output was "analyzed data," which in turn served as input to the client, whose output was "decisions made." Those decisions, in turn served as input to the media staff that placed ads in various media.

The main consequence everyone was trying to achieve was "highest box office receipts for opening weekend." When viewed this way, it is easy to see the relationship of each group's work to that of the others. Before coming to this insight, each team blamed the other for being "so slow," or saw them as "a group of morons," or asked, "Can't anybody get it right anymore?" Once the teams had worked through their group and process models and were able to see their relationship clearly, tensions were reduced. The whole group looked at ways they could support each other in accomplishing the work on time and to the standard of quality needed. The cost of the process was reduced by 10%, and the effectiveness was improved by 20%.

This approach removes much of the emotion that can plague such discussions on work linkage. Stubborn refusal to move forward is avoided because the data about the work is in front of everyone involved, and everyone is looking at the same information. The Work Group Models are the focus of the discussion.

Receiving Team Assignments
 Work Group Model

Have you ever:
- Wanted a way to ask clarifying questions when the team receives a work assignment?
- Wanted a way to make sure all needed information about an assignment is presented at the outset, including management support?

Giving task assignments at the individual level, described previously, is difficult enough. And while the Work Formula can help each supervisor do a better job of giving assignments, it can also help individuals clarify assignments by knowing what to ask.

The order of magnitude increases dramatically when a team is given an assignment which needs to be perceived correctly by everyone on the team in order to be completed successfully. The number of people involved and the scope of the task can cause errors. It can sometimes be seen as a miracle that we do as well as we do in business, industry, and government given that we don't have a common, shared language of work. It's not just a question of you asking, "Did I get that assignment right myself?" or "Did others get it the way I heard it?" Few people are apt to ask such questions, let alone know what to ask, unless they use a commonly shared view and understanding of the team work.

How can a team know that everyone has understood an assignment correctly? Simply begin with the outputs and consequences of the project, task, or assignment. Ensure clarity here, and all further questions will be pertinent and useful. Once the boss has assured agreement with these two elements, then the rest of the assignment can precede much like a planning project.

One of the things you can do to assure that assignments are correctly received is to ask pertinent work-related questions. These work questions should be based, in large part, on the group's Work Model. Ask what inputs are to be used and what conditions are to be followed; ask about the process overall and any steps that need clarifying; then ask what feedback is needed, from whom, and when and how it will be provided. You may also want to ask how management can further support the team, what the milestones will be and when they are to be met. Sometimes these last questions are overlooked, but they are important.

One of our most exciting demonstrations of the power of the Work Group Model occurred when we facilitated model-building for a team of project managers working on the installation of a new, countrywide cellphone system. Eight people would be working with internal and external teams, ensuring that all the work was done on time and on budget. They produced a high-level work model of the whole project, then a next-level model of the work each of the project managers would be supervising. The modeling took about four hours. Then the team reviewed, asked questions, added to the model, coordinated with others, considered their own strengths and weaknesses and built their own model. At the end of the exercise, they told us that they had much more confidence in the success of the project because everyone was looking at the same information at the same time. In fact, the project was indeed successfully implemented.

Managers appreciate being asked questions that do not have a hostile basis. If your management uses the Work Formula to give group assignments, less of this kind of work clarification may be needed. But when the team is asking questions in work-related terms, managers will be encouraged to answer in those terms.

Informing Management (as a Team)
Work Group Model

Getting a work assignment can be greatly enhanced using the Language of Work and it follows that keeping management well informed can be enhanced as well. Keeping management informed takes several different forms, ranging from needs related to product, and service outputs related to status and financial reporting. Here we are concerned principally with how to use the Language of Work to enhance keeping management apprised of progress and results as a team. Thus, since the Work Formula, principally in the form of your Work Group Model, is an accurate and complete definition and measurement of work, it becomes an excellent tool for communicating to management.

As a team, your obligation to inform management generally centers on whether the team is achieving its expected work outputs and attaining the related consequences. If the team is falling short in either of these, the team has an obligation to inform management, but providing negative information is never easy. This conversation, triggered by a failure or potential failure to deliver outputs or achieve consequences, will be easier and less emotional if it begins with an analysis of the sources of the problem. Analysis is not a blame game, but rather an objective look at many of the possible sources:

- Were the inputs available? On time? Of appropriate quality?
- Were there any conditions that kept the team from doing its work?
- What process steps needed more attention?
- Was appropriate feedback available? Provided? Timely?

Once this analysis is completed, then the questions are:
- What could management do to help achieve the outputs and consequences?
- Are the overall work support needs available?
- Are there human relations issues that need attention?
- Is financial support adequate?

To each of these are also the related questions of expected work standards in terms of quality, quantity, timeliness, and cost. The Work Model can also give the team a handle on suggesting solutions, as well as pinpointing problems.

Let's consider a case in which a team was responsible for distributing benefit enrollment cards to 8000 employees, as well as communicating the changes in benefits from the previous year. The importance was great, since the insurance companies had very demanding deadlines. Any delay in the distribution of enrollment cards could have had devastating consequences to employees. Executives were looking closely at the project.

And there were problems. Although the cards were delivered to employees on time, it was not without many hours of overtime and a larger-than-budgeted printing cost. Since this was an annual occurrence, the debriefing that followed included answers shown in Figure 18 to the questions above:

Questions	Answers
Were the inputs available?	NO; the insurer was late in providing premium costs.
On time?	Insurer sent info to Benefits Manager late.
Appropriate quality?	First prices were wrong and had to be revised.
Are there any conditions that keep the team from doing its work?	The Communications Team had to follow the lead of the Benefits Manager.
What process steps need attention?	The interaction with the printing department was weak.
Was appropriate feedback available? Provided? Timely?	Benefits Manager did not see the importance of getting info from insurers correct and timely as part of his job.

Figure 18

Once this non-emotional analysis was shown to the executive team, it was easy to develop a list of action items for continuous improvement of the process. For example, the Senior Vice President for Human Resources met with the insurer to ensure that premium costs would be provided on time and accurately the following year by indicating that a repetition of this year's problem would result in the company choosing a different vendor. The Communications Manager was able to clearly see the need to improve the process between her and the printing department and moved to remedy it. The following year was much less fraught with problems.

Role Relationships on the Team
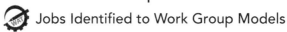 Jobs Identified to Work Group Models

A work group is a team in which each individual knows what his or her job is and how that job relates to others. In the past, all this was intuitive, unseen, and often buried. There has been no way to make these relationships explicit until the advent of Job and Work Group Models using the same definition of work. In their place could be much gossip or personality-based innuendo. Traditionally, the closest to showing interrelationships between jobs in a work group has been the use of flow or swim lane diagrams. But even this fall short because they typically only specify about one-third of what work is. Often there is so much detail that individual work gets confused within the core process, while there is no job relationship among employees in a work group. To the work group modeling you have done already, the authors have added an innovative and powerful tool that makes role relationships on a team abundantly clear.

Once you have modeled the work group, you can name the jobs within the work group, assign a number and/or color to each and identify which jobs have a role in completing each of the process steps leading to work group outputs. This is illustrated in Figure 19.

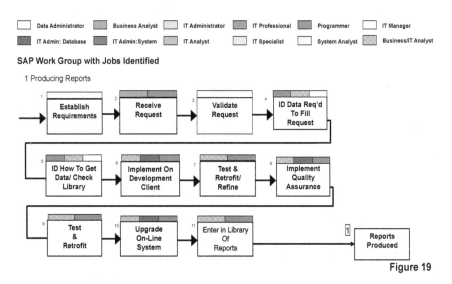

Figure 19

As you see, this diagram clearly shows who on the team is involved in each step of a given process. (This model does not, by itself, constitute a job description or task list. Instead, it shows what roles the individual jobs are "playing" in the process. When more than one employee is involved, it is easy to visualize.)

Thus, in step 4 of the process of Producing Reports, the Programmer, Business Analyst, and Data Administrator all have a role in "Identifying Data Required To Fill Request." If you are, for example, the Programmer, it is quite clear that you have a role in this step and that you share it with others. You can readily see that you are involved in eight of the eleven steps that produce this output and that all the places you work with others are clear.

The 80/20 rule, and our direct observation of work in hundreds of workplaces, reveals that 80% of the problems occur in 20% of the work. Using a process model for role relationships helps to pinpoint precisely where any given problem occurs. Instead of arguing, the team can "vote" to identify the problem. Once identified, it is quite easy to then find the problem, revise the process, or develop procedures to clarify the situation.

Each member of the team can identify his or her sole and joint accountabilities within the team. Stress and drama decline considerably when these maps are used by teams attempting to successfully deliver outputs to others.

For example, the authors were able to use a Work Group Model to create a distinction between two groups with the same job title, but in different departments: Organization Development Specialists (ODS). One of the groups served only one department, while the other served the entire corporation. After we helped them model the groups in each department, it became clear that the corporate-wide ODS actually only facilitated meetings and training sessions. The department-specific group, on the other hand, could be attached to any number of different projects, and their role included data-gathering, analysis, and problem-solving, in addition to facilitation. Once this distinction was understood by everyone, previous rivalry and confusion were eliminated.

[Special note: Although jobs can be attached to Work Group Models to clarify role relationships, it is best to model the whole organization in a certain order. This book in the *Work Trilogy* series—designed to clarify and improve your work as an individual and part of a team—assumes you are not involved in *The Business Model* of the Language of Work. There is a logical, preferred order to modeling and aligning work: first business unit modeling, followed by core process, job, and finally work group modeling. However, the reality is that modeling jobs or the work group often occurs first. This is still a powerful approach, even in its stand-alone form, and the order should not affect the validity of the results.]

Meetings

 Work Formula

It is our experience that entirely too many organizational meetings are full of surprises. Just as employees of a company can regard the same jobs from a different point of view, attendees can go into meetings with very different perspectives on purpose or hoped-for outcomes. We recognize that electronic tools have helped to reduce this chaos, but we find that even the most structured meetings can end up being random and unproductive. If your manager, on the other hand, were to structure most work meetings on the Language of Work, you would find that your role in such meetings can be greatly enhanced. By structuring work meetings on a common understanding of the work and how it is best achieved, everyone knows where the discussion is going, and where and how to contribute.

To reiterate, the Work Formula displays the effect and then the cause of work; it shows the systemic relationship between outputs/ consequences relative to inputs, conditions, process steps, and feedback. Meetings structured on this basis are focused discussions on how to make work more efficient and effective (see the other volumes in *The Work Trilogy* for additional details). Thus, while each job holder and team member reports on results (outputs and consequences), the meeting also explores the processes used and obstacles that prevent achievement. As each person contributes to the status on any project—itself structured on the LoW—each person can easily follow what is being said and comment or suggest improvements based on inputs, conditions, process steps, and feedback. Any related issues of work support, standards, human relations, and financial support can also be addressed coherently and in the context of how they positively or negatively impact work execution. Comments and issues are all relevant in this context.

Team meetings that jump from one topic or issue to another, without resolution, lead to much more confusion and stress than necessary. The LoW simply makes being together as one possible; therefore your meeting structure should be no less well organized, known, and conducted than your daily work itself. Here are some useful guidelines for structuring your meetings:

- Identify first what consequences and outputs need addressing (in Work Group and/or Job Models).
- Identify the focus of reporting or discussion: process steps, inputs, conditions, feedback, and/or work support.
- Identify who will cover each aspect.
- Identify desired changes, if any: Who will make the change and when? Does a work model need to be developed or updated to assure success?
- What are the milestones? Do any dates need to be changed?
- What are the next steps? What feedback is needed, and to whom? When will the next meeting take place?

Problem Solving
AS IS/TO BE

Problem solving has often been an elusive, creative skill. The reality is, however, that problem solving is largely a matter of first getting clarity about the problem itself (its causes and results), then being able to think creatively about how to solve or resolve it. In fact, it's almost impossible to achieve the solution without that clarity. That is where the Work Formula, generally in the form of AS IS/TO BE, comes in. The formula is largely about achieving the indispensable clarity. Here is an example:

An organization we consulted with provided in-home nursing and personal care to residents in three counties (Divisions 1, 2, and 3). The newly hired director had heard about problems from board members, employees, and clients. Various people offered different solutions. What our client needed was an easy way to display the current reality (As Is) and the desired reality (To Be), in order to develop a series of solutions and obtain board approval to proceed. By using the Language of Work as a template, all the observations of the various groups could be laid out in a clear, logical and unemotional way. An example of this is shown in Figure 20 in the form of the WAT we call the AS IS/TO BE table.

Once the director of this organization had laid out the current state of the agency (AS IS), which included input from the employees, it was then possible to describe what should be in place. This is the TO BE state.

The third step is to then determine what to do for each gap between the AS IS and the TO BE. This should be done in a logical

AS IS/TO BE ANALYSIS

PROJECT: In-Home Nursing and Personal Care

	INPUTS	CONDITIONS	PROCESS STEPS	OUTPUTS	CONSEQUENCES	FEEDBACK
AS IS	• Staffing is inadequate in Division • Recruiting & retaining employees difficult • No Mgmt. presence in Division 2 • No Mgmt. present in Division 3	• Funding is limited • Benefits not provided to field staff • BOD does not see funding as its mission • No policy to call-outs • Cost overruns	• Training of field staff is minimal • Inefficiencies slowing work • Duplicate computer systems • Orientation too broad • Limited HR support at Div. 2 &3	• Services offered are limited	• Current reputation is poor • Teamwork is weak • Public unaware of services • Funding is inadequate	• Communication between offices is weak • Recognition of staff is needed
TO BE	• Staffing is good • Employee turnover is low	• Budget is balanced • Field staff get paid vacation & group health access • Board is high functioning • Callouts are minimal • Client changes are controlled	• Field staff well trained • Work is efficient • Systems support works • HR Support works	• New Services successfully added quarterly	• Reputation is great • Team is strong • Public awareness is high	• Communication flows in all directions • Staff feels treasured

© 1999 Performance International

Figure 20

way—addressing the easiest first, and moving on to the more difficult. Research may be needed to find best practices, or consultation with experts. Following the 80/20 rule, 80% of problems can be resolved once each problem is agreed on by all parties. Additional details on Problem Solving using AS IS/TO BE are included in *The Managing Model* and worthy of your review at some point.

Resolving Conflicts
 Models, Matrices

Conflicts in the workplace are usually of two kinds: personal and work-related issues. Much has been written about handing personal issues—in fact, to read training catalogues and offerings for working with difficult people, one would think of the workplace as a hotbed of alienation and dysfunction. All the personality tools, from the DIRT index, through Meyers-Briggs and even the enneagram, are touted to provide understanding of differences in order to reduce personality conflicts.

There is a place for such psychological approaches, but remember rarely is a manager well-trained and certified in resolving issues created by personal agendas, personality differences or deep-seated biases.

But most—if not all—the conflicts that arise because of work (the second cause) can be resolved by using the Language of Work. Having discussions that center on the execution of individual or collective work using appropriate job and/or work group models keeps resolutions focused.

Once the conflict is clearly identified and agreed on, the cause or causes can also be identified. Pinpointing the source of the problem on a black-and-white model allows all parties to generate solutions. Is this a problem in quantity? Quality? Timeliness? Process? Then a solution can be generated as a team: change of resources, change in policy or procedure, discussion among managers, etc.

A feature of the Language of Work Formula that makes conflict resolution possible is that the emotional component of such discussions is likely to be more objective and less "political," which we define here as who is liked/not liked and by whom. When the conflict in work execution is framed in less personal terms, such as

"The inputs are not arriving as soon as I need them" or
"I get inputs in a form that causes me extra work" or
"The rules around here are too restrictive" or
"This part of the process needs improving" and/or
"The communication (work feedback) is missing."

The focus is consistently on the work and making it better, not on complaints, blame, or individuals. Gone is the emotion associated with work problems. Efficient solutions can result quickly.

Conflict can also be related to work support issues (i.e., why the company isn't providing safety training, for example). We have found that, to be seriously addressed such support issues need to be linked to work execution. To reiterate, the LoW keeps conflict resolution centered on the issues at hand.

In conclusion, you see that various work needs are more easily implemented using the variety of ways that the work formula may be structured in the form of appropriate work analytic tools. As you implement these and other individual and team needs you are encouraged to first see how the work formula may be utilized.

Chapter 7

Assuring Continuous Improvement

The LoW is not just a model for defining and clarifying work. It also naturally extends one's thinking through the Work Formula to planning, discussing, reasoning, and improving work. In this chapter we use the Work Formula itself as a Work Application Tool (WAT) for continuous improvement. In the two other books in this series, *The Business Model* and *The Managing Model*, we show management how to use the Work Formula for continuous improvement in a more programmatic way. Here, we extend beyond these programs to describe creating a "mindset" that encourages systems thinking. When you think systematically, you can make improvements in work on your own and with others.

Work is always changing. So it is important to be ready to continuously improve one's work at every level, including that of the individual. The Work Formula will help you and others you work with improve work on an on-going basis.

As the originators of the LoW, we came to recognize that after we introduced a specific application (i.e., reorganization) of the LoW in an organization, workers at multiple levels, including yours, continued to use the LoW in numerous other ways. For instance, they reported that subsequent meetings involved discussion of outputs and consequences; what inputs, conditions, process steps, and feedback led to them; and the use of that information to determine what needed to change. This applied as well to problem solving, planning, conflict resolution, and so forth. The LoW had clearly provided them—as we suggested above—not just a model for defining and clarifying work, but a shared way to plan, discuss, and improve both jobs and processes.

We will here describe "improving work" for you in this more informal, continuing way, while its other, more formal uses for continuous improvement are covered in other books of *The Work Trilogy*.

Continuous improvement—especially in professional, technical, research, engineering, medical, manufacturing, and like fields—is necessary to retain competitiveness and grow businesses. While usually instituted and managed at the managerial level in more formal, programmatic ways, the Work Formula can be used by individuals and at team levels for job enhancement, career resilience, and increasing one's value to the company.

For example: Sometimes, when individuals see their tasks as routine and fully learned, they consider increasing efficiency or productivity as solely management's concern. The subject can come up during a performance review, or after a higher-level meeting about department goals or productivity. If, before either of those circumstances arises, the employee has already used the Work Formula for continuous improvement—making improvements in job execution before a manager asks for them—the employee can be seen as increasingly valuable to the company and may be rewarded accordingly.

By a self-review of your own performance, using the Work Formula on a continuing basis (regardless of the formal process for such a review), thinking about work in a systematic way can become an excellent tool for identifying areas of the job that could be improved. For example, if one of your outputs is someone else's input, seeing how that interrelationship can be improved in terms of both efficiency and effectiveness becomes clear. It may also be a matter of better feedback, attention to the conditions, process steps, or whatever—pinpointed by use of the Work Formula.

In addition to the benefits to the individual, the Work Formula for continuous improvement can be powerful for a team or work group, and for the same reasons: increased efficiency and productivity. Because the users of the formula are easily able to look at work the same way, issues are readily identified and not endlessly discussed. Everyone can address them long before meetings and other formal management programs. The ability to make needed improvement becomes a given—a part of the culture or the "mindset" of the organization.

To help in developing a mindset for improvement, Figures 21 and 22 address continuing improvement by asking how problem-causing situations can be improved. This particular WAT poses

Work Analysis Aid

Page 1 of 2

In General:
The Work Analysis Aid provides a systematic way to use work execution models and support matrices to review and decide needed change in work performance. Sample analysis questions—such as "What is the worth or value of an output?"—to the six elements and layers of work are provided to start your thinking as to how to resolve an identified work problem/need. Pose these questions after determining areas of work improvement from use of the Work Improvement Identification Aid.
You are reminded that there are four ways of changing work: (1) establish, (2) improve, (3) maintain, or (4) extinguish; keep such in mind when proposing work change. Questions are not limited to those listed here; they serve as a beginning to tailoring for your work environment.

WORK EXECUTION

A. First look at **Outputs** and **Consequences** for work results. Ask:
 a) What is the worth (value) of each output to the customer/client?
 b) Is the quality of this output sufficient for the next receiver to use well?
 c) Is the quality in keeping with its cost?
 d) Is it being done by the right person or unit?
 e) Can it be transferred? Consolidated? Outsourced?
 f) Can you reduce the frequency of the delivery of the output?
 g) Can you reduce the number of people receiving the service?
Compare outputs to the consequences.
 h) Are they aligned with each other?
 i) Are any other new outputs needed to satisfy any of the identified consequences?

Answers The Question:
*"How are work problems
to be resolved?*

© 2015 Performance International
Language of Work™   **Figure 21**

B. Look at **Conditions** for cause. Ask:
 a) Are any of the conditions inhibiting successful performance of process steps, use of inputs, or feedback?
 b) Do any conditions need to be modified?
 c) Do any conditions need to eliminated?
 d) Which of the conditions should be reinforced for adherence?
 e) Could management do things to improve specific compliance? Or, remove debilitating conditions?

C. Look at **Process Steps** first for cause. Ask:
 a) Where are the trouble spots in the process steps?
 b) Who can address the trouble spots?
 c) Are there "white spaces" that need to be better managed? (i.e., pass offs that "fall thru the cracks)
 d) What skills and knowledge are needed to complete each step in the process? Which of these need to be further developed?
 e) Is training effectively transferring to job? Would other interventions (i.e. mentoring) be more effective?
 f) Can any of the steps be delegated?
 g) Is the process being conducted by the right person or department?

WORK EXECUTION

Work Analysis Aid

Page 2 of 2

WORK EXECUTION

D. Look at **Inputs** for cause. Ask:
 a) Is the quality of this input sufficient to the do-er?
 b) What form does the input come in? Can the input be systematized? Automated? Organized differently? Consolidated? Do you wait for or go get the output?
 c) Is the input being received by the right person or unit?
 d) Can the waiting time be changed? Reduced?
 e) Is the trigger clearly defined when it comes to you?
 f) What could be done to improve the trigger's clarity?
 g) What resources can be eliminated/ added/modified?

E. Look at **Feedback** for cause. Ask:
 a) What further feedback during process steps is needed?
 b) What feedback is further needed for inputs?
 c) What feedback is further needed for conditions?
 d) What feedback is missing or needed more when the work is finished?
 e) Would a different schedule of reinforcement enhance desired results in inputs, conditions, process steps?
 f) By whom should feedback be improved?
 g) Is a system change needed for feedback?
 h) Are there reports or automated reminders that would provide improved feedback?

Answers The Question:
*"How are work problems
to be resolved?*

© 2015 Performance International
Language of Work™   **Figure 22**

F. Look at **Work Standards** for cause. Ask:
 a) What standards need to be established/clarified?
 b) Are standards ignored to get the work done?
 c) Does the customer have stated/clear standard expectations?

G. Look at **Work Support** for cause. Ask:
 a) What interventions, at what level, need improving or are missing?
 b) What new interventions would improve work?
 c) What interventions could be eliminated?
 d) Are any interventions being ignored?
 e) Do any interventions cause a barrier to work performance?

H. Look at **Human Relations** for cause. Ask:
 a) What human relations factors are getting in the way of getting the work accomplished?
 b) Does the human relations factor require professional help to fix?
 c) Could policy changes improve Human Relations factors?

I. Look at **Financial Support** for cause. Ask:
 a) What additional financial support is needed?
 b) Is training require in financial literacy?
 c) What additional financial support needs to be brought to the attention of senior management?

ORGANIZATIONAL SUPPORT

a series of questions which can be answered individually or as a group. Answers—or "what to do"—are embedded in the "Cause" questions. We have found that the use of this tool can uniformly solve issues of need, especially when doing so in groups.

These are the kinds of questions that we, as developers and experts in the LoW, have instinctually developed and used over the years in our consulting engagements because we are constantly employing the Work Formula. Your repeated use over time will help create throughout the company a "mindset for continuous improvement" that supports a business's choices which allow it to grow and compete in the marketplace.

We hope that you, your managers, and the executives would use these questions along with the various other Work Analytic Tools to improve work continuously and systematically. If you do, you will find they become second-nature in your analysis, implementation, and improvement of all ongoing work. This is the mindset we hope for.

Should you want to read a more extensive discussion of this particular aid, you will find it in *The Managing Model*.

In closing, we hope this book, as part of our *Work Trilogy* series, will encourage increasingly effective business practices and workplaces, with increasingly capable and enthusiastic performers.

Language of Work Terminology

Continuous Improvement Mindset

The natural extension of the Language of Work to improve work growing out of a fundamental understanding and use of a Work Formula. One of three goals of the Language of Work.

Financial Support Matrix

This matrix extends the application of the Language of Work formula to identify the financials an organization needs to support work execution.

Human Relations Matrix

This matrix extends the Language of Work formula to the areas of human interaction necessary to support work execution.

Language of Work

A systemic, enterprisewide behavioral model, based on the Work Formula, that integrates organizing, managing, implementing, and continuously improving work. In so doing it establishes a way to achieve alignment, transparency, and continuous improvement throughout an organization.

Work Alignment

Use of a Work Formula to ensure that work between different levels is in keeping with the goals and desired consequences of the organization. One of three goals of the Language of Work.

Work Analytic Tools

A variety of ways to use the Work Formula. Can be used to choose approaches for applying the Language of Work formula.

Work Analytics

The process used to analyze work. In the Language of Work, it is the Work Formula.

Work Formula

The six systemic elements that make up work: Inputs, Conditions, Process Steps, Outputs, Consequences, and Feedback.

Work Layer

Those aspects of work that promote and sustain work execution: Standards, Work Support (aka culture), Human Relations, and Financial Support. In the LoW, each of these is represented by a matrix.

Work Level

The Language of Work formula is applied to the four arenas where work is executed: business units, core processes, jobs, and work groups.

Work Matrices

The graphic representation of Work Layers using the Work Formula on one axis and the Levels of Work on the other. Each cell is populated with programs, services, and interventions (or change processes) provided by the organization to support work execution.

Work Models

Graphic flow diagrams based on the elements of the Work Formula. When populated with data from the appropriate work level, they show the work of business units, core processes, jobs, and work groups.

Work Standards Matrix

This matrix extends the Language of Work formula to standards to which work execution should rise in terms of quality, quantity, timeliness, and cost.

Work Support Matrix

The cultural provisions provided by an organization in direct support of work execution at the business unit, core processes, jobs, and work group levels.

Work Transparency

Assuring that the organization's work is clearly defined and understood by everyone at each Work Level and Layer. No secrets in the work. One of three goals of the Language of Work.

Language of Work Implementation Models

The *Working Model* has been addressed in this eBook. The *Business Model* and the *Managing Model* are addressed in the two other eBooks of *The Work Trilogy*.

The following are the three major Work Implementation Models of the Language of Work. These are followed by a list of Organizational Effectiveness techniques that can use the Language of Work to improve their overall efficiency and effectiveness. You may access definitions, articles, case studies, books, and other information, including certification, at our website: www.performanceinternational.com

Language of Work

The Business Model

For Executives

Work Formula

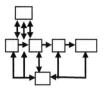

1. Business Unit Model
2. Core Process Models
3. Job Models
4. Work Group Models
5. Work Standards Matrix
6. Work Support Matrix
7. Human Relations Matrix
8. Financial Support Matrix

TO ACHIEVE:
- Work Alignment
- Transparency
- Continuous Improvement

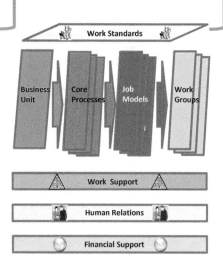

Language of Work
The Managing Model

For Managers

TO ACHIEVE:
- Work Facilitation Alignment
- Transparency
- Continuous Improvement

9. Planning Work
10. Linking With Other Groups
11. Selecting Employees
12. Job/Work Group Orientation
13. Establishing Systems
14. Assigning Tasks
15. Facilitating Work
16. Reinforcing Work Performance
17. Training & Work Performance
18. Facilitating Change
19. Facilitating Work Support
20. Informing Management
21. Job & Work Group Models
22. Assuring Role Relationships
23. Conducting Meetings
24. Improving Quality
25. Problem Solving
26. Resolving Conflicts
27. Measuring Work
28. Transferring Knowledge
29. Reviewing Performance
30. Career Development

Work Formula

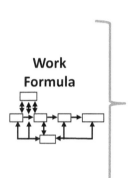

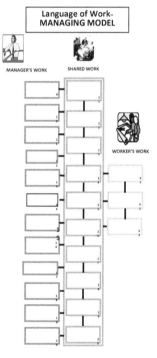

Language of Work–
MANAGING MODEL

MANAGER'S WORK   SHARED WORK

WORKER'S WORK

Language of Work

The Working Model

For Individual Worker and Team

Work Formula

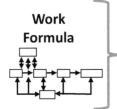

31. **Work Implementation**
32. **Continuous Work Improvement**

TO ACHIEVE:
- Work Alignment
- Transparency
- Continuous Improvement

Organizational Effectiveness interventions that may be enhanced by use of the Language of Work Model:

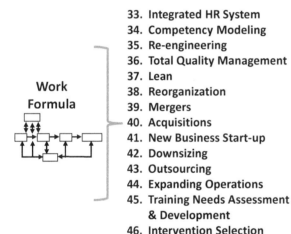

Language of Work
Organizational Effectiveness

For:
Change Agents,
Performance
Consultants,
Trainers, HR, etc

Work Formula

33. Integrated HR System
34. Competency Modeling
35. Re-engineering
36. Total Quality Management
37. Lean
38. Reorganization
39. Mergers
40. Acquisitions
41. New Business Start-up
42. Downsizing
43. Outsourcing
44. Expanding Operations
45. Training Needs Assessment & Development
46. Intervention Selection
47. Job Descriptions
48. Identifying & Loading Jobs to Core Processes

TO ACHIEVE:
• Systems Approach based on LoW
• Consistency with LoW Models

PERFORMANCE
INTERNATIONAL

References

Hammer, Michael and James Champy. (1993) *Reengineering The Corporation*. New York: Harper-Collins.

Kolbe, K. (2003). *Powered By Instinct*. Phoenix, AZ: Monuments Press.

Langdon, Danny G. (2000). *Aligning Performance: Improving People, systems and Organizations*. San Francisco, CA: Jossey-Bass/Pheiffer Publishers.

Langdon, Danny G. (1995). *The New Language of Work*. Amherst, MA: HRD Press.

Langdon, Danny G. and Kathleen Whiteside, *Bringing Sense to Competency Definition and Attainment*, ISPI, Performance Improvement, vol. 43-7, 2004.

Langdon, Danny G., Kathleen Langdon, Johnilee Whiteside, (2014). *Righting the Enterprise – A Primer for Organizing or Reorganizing the Right Way*. Bellingham, WA: Performance International (free from our website at: http://lnkd.in/d66wnjb or in other formats at: https://www.smashwords.com/books/view/431840

Langdon, Danny G. (2001). *Should We Conduct Cause Analysis or Change of State Analysis*, ISPI, Performance Improvement, October, 2003, pp 8-13.

J. Robert Carlton and Claude S. Lineberry (2004). *Achieving Post-Merger Success*. San Francisco, CA: Jossey-Bass/Pheiffer Publishers.

Rummler, Geary A., and Alan P Brache. (1990) *Improving Performance: How to Manage the White Space on the Organization Chart* (2nd ed.). San Francisco, CA: Jossey-Bass/Pheiffer Publishers (p. 64).

Books by the Authors

Langdon, Danny G. (1995), *The New Language of Work*. Amherst, MA: HRD Press.

Langdon, Danny G. (2000). *Aligning performance: Improving people, systems and organizations*. San Francisco, CA: Jossey-Bass/Pheiffer Publishers.

Langdon, Danny G., Kathleen Whiteside, and Monica McKenna. (1999). *Interventions Resource Guide: 50 Performance Improvement Tools*. San Francisco, CA: Jossey-Bass/Pheiffer Publishers.

Langdon, Danny G., Kathleen Langdon, Johnilee Whiteside, (2014). *Righting the Enterprise – A Primer for Organizing or Reorganizing the Right Way*. Bellingham, Wa: Performance International (free from our website at: http://lnkd.in/d66wnjb or in other formats at: https://www.smashwords.com/books/view/431840

Langdon, Danny G. and Kathleen Langdon. (2018) The Work Trilogy: The Business Model: Using The Language of Work To Organize and Align Work, Bellingham, WA: Performance International, www.performanceinternational.com.

Langdon, Danny G. and Kathleen Langdon. (2018) The Work Trilogy: The Managing Model: Using The Language of Work To Facilitate Work, Bellingham, WA: Performance International, www.performanceinternational.com.

Langdon, Danny G. and Kathleen Langdon. (2018) The Work Trilogy: The Working Model: Using The Language of Work To Implement Work, Bellingham, WA: Performance International, www.performanceinternational.com.

Author Biographies

Danny G. Langdon, Co-founder of Performance International, with forty+ years' experience, has published twelve books, and served as the series editor of the 40-volume "Instructional Designs Library." He is the recipient of three major ISPI awards of excellence, a past international president, and Honorary Life Member. He is the originator of the Language of Work Model™,  and has presented at more than 35 international conferences, published numerous articles, and conducted numerous workshops.

Kathleen Langdon, Co-founder of Performance International, has served external clients for more than thirty years, concentrating on embedding work performance improvement in numerous companies. She served as Corporate Director of Human Resources for a major service medical organization. She is a past president of ISPI, invited speaker for the annual ISPI Awards Banquet,  and led 15 business executives to explain performance technology to the White House. She is the co-editor of "Intervention Resource Guide: 50 Performance Improvement Tools," published numerous articles, and is a frequent presenter at conferences here and abroad.

CPSIA information can be obtained
at www.ICGtesting.com
Printed in the USA
FSHW01n0210060818
51036FS